ACADEMIC INTEGRITY MATTERS

edited by
DANA D. BURNETT
LYNN RUDOLPH
KAREN O. CLIFFORD

National Association of Student
Personnel Administrators, Inc.

Academic Integrity Matters. Copyright © 1998 by the National Association of Student Personnel Administrators, Inc. Printed and bound in the United States of America. All rights reserved. No part of this book may be reproduced in any form or by any electronic or mechanical means without written permission from the publisher. First edition.

NASPA does not discriminate on the basis of race, color, national origin, religion, sex, age, affectional or sexual orientation, or disability in any of its policies, programs, and services.

Library of Congress
Cataloging-in-Publication Data
Academic integrity matters / edited by Dana D. Burnett, Lynn Rudolph, Karen O. Clifford.
    p.   cm.
    ISBN 0-931654-23-8
    1. Cheating (Education)—United States. 2. College students—United States—Conduct of life. 3. Education, Higher—Moral and ethical aspects—United States. I. Burnett, Dana D. II. Rudolph, Lynn. III. Clifford, Karen O. IV. National Association of Student Personnel Administrators (U.S.)
    LB3609.A29   1998   97-51743
    378.1'98—dc21   CIP

MONOGRAPH SERIES EDITORIAL BOARD

Margaret Healy, *editor*
Mankato State University
Mankato, Minnesota

Marianne Bock
Kent State University
Kent, Ohio

Kristine E. Dillon
University of Southern California
Los Angeles, California

Sandy Estanek
Alvernia College
Reading, Pennsylvania

Barbara Henley
University of Illinois-Chicago
Chicago, Illinois

Debora Liddell
University of Iowa
Iowa City, Iowa

Maureen A. McCarthy
Austin Peay University
Clarksville, Tennessee

Susan E. Mitchell
California State University
San Marcos, California

Robbie Nayman
Fullerton, California

Bettina Shuford
Bowling Green State University
Bowling Green, Ohio

OTHER NASPA MONOGRAPH TITLES

Advice from the Dean: A Personal Perspective on the Philosophy, Roles, and Approaches of a Dean at a Small, Private, Liberal Arts College

A Student Affairs Guide to the ADA and Disability Issues

Different Voices: Gender and Perspective in Student Affairs Administration

Diversity, Disunity, and Campus Community

From Survival to Success: Promoting Minority Student Retention

The Invisible Leaders: Student Affairs Mid-Managers

Life at the Edge of the Wave: Lessons from the Community College

The New Professional: A Resource Guide for New Student Affairs Professionals and Their Supervisors

Puzzles and Pieces in Wonderland: The Promise and Practice of Student Affairs Research

The Role of Student Affairs in Institution-Wide Enrollment Management Strategies

Student Affairs and Campus Dissent: Reflection of the Past and Challenge for the Future

Working with International Students and Scholars on American Campus

NASPA's monographs may be purchased by contacting NASPA at 1875 Connecticut Avenue, NW, Suite 418, Washington, D.C. 20009-5728; 202-265-7500 (tel.) or 202-797-1157 (fax).

CONTENTS

Preface   vii

Chapter 1   *1*
Creating a Campus Climate for Academic Integrity
    Jon C. Dalton

Chapter 2   *13*
Students' Perceptions of Academic Integrity: Curtailing Violations
    Wanda Kaplan and Phyllis Mable

Chapter 3   *23*
The Academic Dishonesty of College Students: The Prevalence of the Problem and Effective Educational Prevention Programs
    William L. Kibler

Chapter 4   *39*
The Classroom Environment and Academic Integrity: A Behavioral Science Perspective
    Bernard E. Whitley, Jr., and Mary E. Kite

Chapter 5   *57*
A Comprehensive Approach for Creating a Campus Climate That Promotes Academic Integrity
    Lynn Rudolph and Linda Timm

Chapter 6   *77*
When Institutions and Their Faculty Address Issues of Academic Dishonesty: Realities and Myths
    Donald D. Gehring

Chapter 7   *93*
The Effect of Institutional Policies and Procedures on Academic Integrity
    Donald L. McCabe and Gary M. Pavela

Chapter 8   109
Academic Integrity and Campus Climate at Small Colleges
   Karen O. Clifford

Chapter 9   125
Can the Academic Integrity of Cost-Effective Distance Learning Course Offerings be Protected?
   Mary Elisabeth Randall

Chapter 10   135
The Impact of Technology on Academic Integrity
   Harold Goldsmith

Conclusions   143

Contributors   147

PREFACE

There is a problem festering within our institutions of higher education that threatens to weaken their very foundations. The problem is more threatening than faculty-administration disputes; more costly than the recent and pervasive funding cutbacks; and has a greater potential of eroding the core of the teaching-learning process than underprepared students or overpopulated classrooms. The problem is academic dishonesty, and the need to address the problem is paramount.

On a few campuses, a student-managed honor system is the sole mechanism for enforcing the integrity of the academic process within that academic community. Normative student behavior within these student bodies is presumably such that violations of the honor code are thought to be rare, and when they occur they are often dealt with by dismissal from the institution.

Recently, a steady stream of research articles and news reports suggests that breaches of the precepts of academic integrity may be the rule rather than the exception on college campuses across the nation. Some of these authors conclude that the preoccupation of success within the value systems of contemporary undergraduates is responsible. According to some researchers, students report they view cheating as a means, similar to studying, of obtaining the information necessary to earn a passing grade. Most students indicate they would not report an observed incident of cheating, even if required to do so by an honor code.

What percentage of entering freshman students cheated in high school? How formidable a task do student affairs professionals and faculty have if these entering students are to be educated about their responsibilities for adhering to norms of academic integrity? What empirically derived data can be presented to describe the prevalence of cheating on our campuses? Have any educational programs proven to be effective in curtailing incidents of cheating on campus?

What can be done to manage the classroom environment to curtail the frequency of student cheating? Why do faculty often seem reluctant to confront suspected student cheating? What are the legal implications for faculty and the institution of using grade sanctions without regard to the institutional judicial process to punish students suspected of cheating?

What institutional policies related to academic dishonesty have proven to be effective? Are incidents of cheating fewer on campuses with honor systems? What role should honor councils and other peer groups play in managing academic integrity? How can academic dishonesty policies be designed to be proactive rather than reactive so that optimum communication to students and faculty about academic integrity issues occurs?

The growth of distance learning educational modalities raises questions about how the academic integrity of these cost-efficient course offerings can be protected. How can academic integrity be assured in such a relatively uncontrolled classroom environment? As the educational process becomes more intertwined with technology, defining and recognizing instances of academic dishonesty have become more complex. How can the special circumstances created by the increased use of technology in the teaching, learning, and testing process be managed by those faculty and student affairs professionals who do not comprehend the technological jargon or conceptualize the means for cheating provided by technology?

What do students perceive to be the most effective way of curtailing violations of academic integrity? What can we learn about student cheating behavior from students themselves? And when a preponderance of the evidence indicates that a student has cheated, what sanctions will be the most effective?

This monograph was created to answer these important questions about academic integrity. It is designed to be read by a broad cross-section of our institutional communities. It is the editors, hope that the contents of this volume will serve as a valuable reference, which contains a thorough examination of the many perspectives the problem presents. The ideas and information presented by the monograph's writers can also serve as a catalyst to generate needed and often absent discussion focused on the critical issues surrounding academic integrity on each of our campuses. And it is hoped that the conclusions the reader can draw from the ideas and concepts presented here will lead to successful, fresh interventions.

CREATING A CAMPUS CLIMATE FOR ACADEMIC INTEGRITY

JON C. DALTON

This journey begins with a basic discussion of the values that undergird student behavior. Dalton discusses three strategies for dealing with academic dishonesty and each strategy's role in creating a "culture of academic integrity."

Academic integrity is without question the cornerstone ethical standard in higher education. While educators may debate the role which colleges and universities play in the values education of students, there is little debate that academic integrity is the quintessential moral virtue of the academic community. Teaching and learning depend upon the bedrock ethical integrity of teachers and students to honor the truth and to engage in the pursuit of truth with scrupulous honesty. When students or faculty violate this moral standard, they jeopardize the core integrity of the learning enterprise. No college or university can tolerate the loss of its fundamental ethical credibility.

Despite the crucial importance of academic integrity to higher education, cheating by college students has been a perennial problem. Each generation of educators has struggled with student cheating scandals and sought to develop preventive rules and sanctions to control the persistent problem of academic dishonesty. Some might believe that college cheating only involves the marginal student who cheats to compensate for poor study habits or lack of ability. But empirical evidence suggests that cheating has become so widespread that many of the best students believe cheating is necessary in order to keep a competitive edge.

Much recent research on student cheating indicates that the problem has worsened and become widespread among college students. In a 1992 survey reported by McCabe and Cole (1995), more than half of MIT undergraduates acknowledged that they had collaborated on homework even when the instructor asked for individual work.

What has created this situation and what can colleges and universities do to address the problem? What role do the values of contemporary college students and the peer culture play in creating and perpetuating this problem? How can colleges and universities create a culture of integrity on campus that actively discourages cheating and dishonesty? These and other issues will be examined in this chapter.

THE VALUES OF CONTEMPORARY COLLEGE STUDENTS

Much has been written (Astin, 1993; Levine, 1976) about the utilitarian and materialistic values of contemporary college students. The longitudinal data on first-time-in-college students collected by Alexander Astin and associates indicates a long trend line of increasing concern about money and status among college students and declining interest in education for its own intrinsic personal worth. Although the materialistic interests of college students have begun to level off in recent years (Astin, 1994), it is clear that the overriding priorities of today's college students are to regard higher education as a gateway to future financial and status rewards. Moreover, economic downsizing and increasing competition for jobs and access to graduate and professional schools have fueled the pressure for good grades and academic success among today's college students.

For many students, college is the primary gateway to the "good life" of material rewards and status. The self-interested values of much of collegiate peer culture today support a utilitarian approach to personal ethics, which condones cheating as a necessary means to a desirable end. Bloy (1980) is perhaps too harsh in his description of collegiate peer culture values as the values of the "solitary predator" but he does justly criticize the peer culture for its negative effects on the moral conduct of college students, including academic dishonesty. Consequently, the pressure on students to do well academically has seldom been greater and creates a milieu in which students often feel compelled to achieve good grades by whatever means necessary.

The traditional social prohibitions against cheating appear to have weakened in their influence on college students. Although it is difficult to measure the changing influence of family, religious institutions, and other character building institutions on today's youth in any objective way, there is considerable concern by educators that today's students come to college with less ethical training and guidance. The combination of increased academic competition, condoning peer culture, and weakened character education makes today's college students more susceptible to the problems of academic dishonesty.

THE ETHICAL ETHOS OF CAMPUS LIFE

Public concern about the character building influence of higher education is greater now than in many decades. Problems with college student cheating, acts of racial discrimination on campus, increasing materialism and privatism, a poor work ethic, and the need for more personal commitment to civic responsibility have persuaded public leaders and educators that more must be done in higher education to promote ethical integrity and moral responsibility in students.

The widely acclaimed Wingspread (1993) report on higher education argued that educational reform must include more attention to the place of values in the education of college students and the management of higher education institutions. The report is especially critical of the value neutrality so characteristic of contemporary campus life in which educators avoid the active promulgation of ethical values and norms. The report recommended that higher education adopt a more proactive stance with respect to values education because there has been a general erosion of societal core values and the structures of family and church have less influence with youth today.

Many colleges and universities have attempted to address the concern about values education through the articulation of specific values and character traits that are goals of the curriculum and student life experiences.

The values and character traits most commonly stressed by colleges and universities derive from community norms such as respect for others, fairness, service to others, and truthfulness.

Concern about the moral education of youth has led some educators to push for specific character-building efforts. Barber (1992) argued that public institutions, in particular, have an obligation to promote civic values and social responsibility since education for life in a democratic society requires the skills and commitments of citizenship. According to Barber, the teaching of democratic virtues such as altruism, concern for the common good, and public service are indispensable values for the educated citizen. Truth-telling and personal honesty are, in particular, essential traits of character in a democratic community. Public colleges and universities that do not actively inculcate these values in students produce graduates who are incapable or unwilling to preserve democratic institutions and deal with the pressing moral problems of a pluralistic democratic society.

Colleges and universities create unique normative structures or "moral cultures" for their students as ways of instilling particular ethical values. Some institutions with military traditions such as Virginia Military Institute, the U.S. Naval Academy, and the Citadel, for example, seek to create a disciplined student lifestyle, which directly structures much of students' experiences and transmits specific moral norms. Other schools, such as the University of Virginia, have created special traditions around an Honor Code which is a central feature of academic and student life and an important means of transmitting and regulating standards of academic integrity. Some colleges, Berea College for example, use student employment and a strong work ethic to instill values of solidarity, respect, and moral integrity. Other institutions, particularly large ones, have less regulated student life environments and no special customs or traditions that emphasize academic integrity. It is important to recognize these institutional differences when examining academic integrity; the characteristics of campus culture and moral climate play a very important role in understanding the problem of student cheating and how it ought to be addressed in specific situations.

CAN COLLEGE STUDENTS BE TAUGHT ETHICAL INTEGRITY?

The problem of widespread cheating in college, despite considerable efforts over long periods of time to prevent it, raises the question of whether college students in their late teens and twenties are simply too old to learn ethical behavior. Are the circumstances of testing and evaluation in college so conducive to cheating that practical preventive measures are simply ineffective? Unfortunately, the pervasive and long-standing problem of student cheating leads many educators to conclude that there is no real solution to this problem, only containment of it. Such cynicism about the problem is one of the first hurdles in addressing the problem of academic dishonesty.

Ethical values can be taught. Erikson (1968) believed that late adolescence was the period of life most open to ideological and ethical challenge. Youth is the time for establishing identity, and ethical commitments and values are intrinsic elements of that identity formation. There is no time in the human life cycle more strategic for shaping the norms of the moral vision than young adulthood (Piper, Gentile & Parks, 1993). Moral development can continue into young adulthood if the circumstances in the college environment are right for promoting moral consciousness and commitment.

Cheating should not be accepted as an inevitability among college students. Instead we must examine the nature of our efforts in higher education to teach values related to academic integrity and to actively promote ethical conduct. While many colleges and universities make lofty pronouncements about the ethical outcomes they seek to promote in their students, there is little compelling evidence that institutions have specific educational interventions designed to promote these outcomes (Hastings Foundation, 1980). This chapter examines some of the issues related to promoting ethical development in college students.

THE NATURE OF PEER CULTURE — WHY CHEATING IS CONDONED

The research on the influence of college peers on cheating behaviors suggests that student peers do not always condemn cheating and may even encourage it. Barnett and Dalton (1981) found that students are very reluctant to report cheating and disagree with faculty about what constitutes cheating. Cheating is a term that refers to a wide variety of behaviors that are regarded as unethical. Students have different standards for different kinds of cheating. Their definitions for what constitutes cheating are less rigorous than those of faculty and more open to situational factors. Even faculty disagree about standards that define cheating and thus may send mixed and confusing messages to students.

One of the most important reasons students ignore and even condone peer cheating is that they recognize the great pressure and competition that all students face and empathize with those who cheat as a coping mechanism. This is not to say that college students condone cheating but that they know personally how easily such behavior can occur, given the great pressure present in the collegiate environment. This is the primary reason why so few students ever report cheating. Competition and pressure for good grades are primary reasons for cheating. Faculty, however, do not generally appreciate the extent to which such pressure influences students' behavior. Efforts to reduce cheating must consider these factors since they have such great influence on the peer culture.

Research on student moral development indicates that one of the reasons why situational factors such as test environment and student stress are so important is that even students with high levels of moral judgment will cheat in high-stress test situations in which there is little threat of being caught. Students who reason at high moral judgment levels do not necessarily have strong moral will power and may be as prone to cheat as students at lower stages of moral reasoning in low threat-high stress situations. The test environment is, therefore, the single most important ingredient in controlling cheating behavior.

The prevalence of student cheating can, in part, be attributed to the poorly defined and administered academic integrity standards and test environments that are found in many classrooms. Students entering the collegiate environment do not know the special definitions and expectations of academic integrity at the college level. Most colleges do not provide an extensive orientation to the ethics of scholarship and moral conduct in the academic arena. Students hear strongly worded admonitions about academic cheating and receive statements and rules about behavioral expectations; however, they seldom get the opportunity to discuss the meaning of academic integrity and to explore practical situations involving the ethics of scholarship, which they may encounter in college. Consequently, it is the peer culture that gives most new students their most intensive and practical orientation to academic ethics in college.

THE INSULATION OF THE PEER CULTURE

Since college peers are the biggest single influence on college students (Pascarella & Terenzini, 1991), the challenge for colleges and universities is to develop effective strategies for influencing the peer culture. Yet the dilemma is that it is almost impossible for educational leaders to directly influence the peer culture. So much of what students do in their peer interactions occurs outside the formal activities of the institution. Student culture is shaped in large part by extra-institutional factors such as social groups, entertainment activities, private living arrangements, alcohol and drug usage, work, and personal interests and involvements.

In earlier times it was possible to control and even shape college student culture because of the relative isolation of campuses and smaller numbers of students. Contemporary technology, increasingly urbanized campuses, and larger student bodies provide nearly overwhelming challenges for those who attempt to shape the peer culture. Students are bombarded with multiple value systems and moral influences from sources over which the college has almost no influence. These values and moral influences often run directly counter to what the institution seeks to promote, particularly with respect to academic honesty. The rules say "never cheat," but the peer culture says "sometimes cheating is necessary." The institution says, "honesty is the responsibility of each student." The peer culture says, "Don't blame me if the instructor doesn't monitor and enforce testing situations." The rules say, "report cheating," but the peer culture says "never fink on a fellow student." The reality is that in a contest between institutional and student culture, the influence of the student culture will win every time.

This does not mean that there is little or nothing that can be done to influence student culture on the matter of student cheating. It does mean that institutions must adopt intentional strategies that address and counter the factors that support and condone cheating behavior.

HISTORICAL APPROACHES FOR DEALING WITH CHEATING

Colleges and universities have successfully utilized several types of strategies for dealing with cheating problems. One strategy emphasizes rules, penalties, and punishments. This strategy is based upon the belief that threat and punishment are essential deterrents to cheating behavior and must be instituted in community conduct standards through rules and regulations. From the very beginning of higher education in the United States, colleges have made use of such conduct regulations and have strictly punished students who engaged in academic dishonesty. This strategy remains an important method for dealing with academic dishonesty in many colleges and universities.

Another common strategy for dealing with academic dishonesty is moral education and character development. This strategy is based upon the premise that students can be taught academic integrity through various educational activities designed to promote moral character and ethical responsibility. Schools that emphasize character development emphasize the transmission of values through the curriculum, through structured student life experiences that provide opportunities for moral action and reflection, and through interaction with individuals who serve as moral exemplars. Cheating is regarded as one of many moral conduct problems that can occur if students do not possess strong moral character and the will to act in an ethically responsible manner. No doubt most colleges and universities use some combination of the two strategies discussed above for addressing college cheating.

A third approach to addressing cheating focuses on the intentional design of situational or environmental factors. Advocates of this approach stress that much, if not most, college cheating occurs because there are often few if any barriers or deterrents to the behavior. Thus, cheating happens because "the opportunity is there" and the risks for such behavior are perceived to be very low. Advocates of this approach argue that much college cheating is primarily opportunistic and can be prevented through clear instructions and a well-conceived, deliberately structured, closely-monitored testing environment. Cheating is almost always minimized when there is a consistent pattern of clearly defined expectations coupled with a well administered testing environment, which is consistently monitored for violations.

Controlling for situational or environmental factors is often problematic in higher education because of the decentralized nature of education and educational testing. Faculty typically are very independent in their approaches to teaching and educational evaluation, and college students encounter a wide variety of testing and evaluation situations. Moreover, faculty vary considerably in the attention they give to structuring and monitoring testing situations, so students confront great variation in the circumstances of testing and evaluation during the collegiate experience. No amount of threat or moral education will effectively address student cheating so long as the environment affords easy opportunities for this behavior. Some of the most important environmental steps to deter cheating include: clear instructions, seating arrangements, sufficient test monitors, and alternative test forms.

Each of these three approaches — threat and consequences, moral education, and control of the testing environment — plays an important role in deterring college student cheating. A comprehensive institutional academic integrity policy should therefore include provisions for: (1) cheating definitions, rules, and sanctions (2) moral education and (3) management of environmental and situational factors.

CREATING A CULTURE OF ACADEMIC INTEGRITY

Former Harvard president Derek Bok (1976) argued that teaching ethical values is an inescapable priority for colleges and universities. Piper, Gentile, and Parks (1993) concurred that, "A university that refuses to take ethical dilemmas seriously violates its basic obligation to society." One of the primary tasks of leadership in higher education is to create an ethical climate in which academic integrity is actively promoted and supported.

Students learn ethical conduct in the university in much the same manner they learn conduct in the family setting — through education, role modeling, positive reinforcement, clearly defined standards, and reasonable penalties for failure to meet standards. Unfortunately, in institutional settings it is difficult to provide the personal settings so important for many of these approaches; consequently, institutions depend heavily on promulgating rules and standards and punishing student conduct violations. Thus, much of the moral awareness and persuasion that are instilled through education, role modeling, and positive reinforcement are not conveyed to students, and they confront only rules and sanctions that have little moral meaning for them.

In the highly situational and relative context of students' world of morality in the peer culture, college rules and sanctions have little moral meaning. These rules assume moral meaning in the personal lives of students' struggles to survive and to succeed. This personal realm of moral struggle and adjustment is heavily influenced by peers who share common experiences, who empathize, and who do not judge.

CONCLUSIONS

The question of who has responsibility for setting community standards on campus is a tricky one. Clearly the peer culture has the power to trump any effort on the part of administrators and faculty to promulgate ethical standards, particularly when such standards are perceived as divorced and irrelevant to the circumstances and moral struggles in students' lives. Consequently, it is important that the community of students, faculty, and administrators be involved together in establishing and maintaining ethical standards on campus. It is particularly important that students be actively involved in establishing and maintaining academic integrity standards so that the process reflects students' experiences and concerns and avoids the perception of edict.

To influence students' ethical conduct, colleges and universities must actively promote the value of academic integrity; help students, particularly new ones, to understand its importance in the learning environment; celebrate its special legacy and exemplary role models; and demonstrate the rewards of practicing ethical conduct. This monograph presents and explores strategies designed to alter the campus environment to reduce student cheating and to promote moral awareness and commitment.

References

Astin, A. (1993). *What matters in college.* San Francisco: Jossey-Bass, Inc.

Astin, A.W. (1994). *The American freshman: National norms for fall 1994.* Los Angeles: University of California, Higher Education Research Institute.

Barber, B. (1992). *An aristocracy of everyone: The politics of education and the future of America.* New York: Ballantine Books.

Barnett, D.C., and Dalton, J.C. (1981). "Why college students cheat." *Journal of College Student Personnel, 22,* 545-551.

Bloy, M. (1980). "What students really learn in college." *Newsletter of the National Campus Ministry Institute.* Boston: National Campus Ministry Institute.

Bok, D.C. (1976). "Can ethics be taught?" *Change,* 26-30.

Erikson, E. (1968). *Identity: Youth and crisis.* New York: W. W. Norton and Company.

Hastings Foundation. (1980). *The teaching of ethics in higher education.* New York: author.

Levine, A. (1976). *When dreams and heroes died.* San Francisco: Jossey-Bass, Inc.

McCabe, D.L., and Cole, S. (November 1995). "Student collaboration: Not always what the instructor wants," *AAHE Bulletin.*

Pascarella, E.T., and Terenzini, P.J. (1991). *How college affects students.* San Francisco: Jossey-Bass, Inc.

Piper, T.R., Gentile, M.C., and Parks, S.D. (1993). *Can ethics be taught?* Boston: Harvard Business School.

Wingspread Group on Higher Education. (1993). *An open letter to those concerned about the American future.* Racine, Wisconsin: The Johnson Foundation, Inc.

STUDENTS' PERCEPTIONS OF ACADEMIC INTEGRITY

Curtailing Violations

WANDA KAPLAN
PHYLLIS MABLE

Conventional wisdom provides insight about the challenges that lie ahead for those responsible for academic integrity policy and programs. Mable and Kaplan summarize student focus group data characterizing student views about academic integrity issues at ten U.S. institutions. Their chapter incorporates student commentary into conclusions and recommendations appropriate for policy makers and administrators of academic integrity policy.

Essential to any comprehensive discussion of academic integrity is an examination of students' perceptions of the issues. Focus groups were conducted on ten campuses; students discussed the concept of academic integrity along with its standard, importance, value, meaning, and policy. The focus groups were taped, and they serve as the basis for the content and direction of this chapter.

Colleges and universities participating in the focus groups represent small and large, public and private, two-year and four-year institutions. From this selection of students' views, common themes emerged. Students and campuses were selected to provide a diverse sample of student viewpoints. Table 1 displays the profile of the focus group participants. Students' conversations and critiques are visionary and focused on the head and heart of academic integrity as viewed and understood in the student culture. Students' direct quotes appear in italics.

Table 1
Profile Characteristics for Student Participants and Institutions

Gender
Female   40
Male   44

Class Level
Freshman   7
Sophomore   18
Junior   23
Senior   24
Graduate/Professional   11

Age
18-24   71
25 and over   13

Ethnicity/Race
African-American   14
Asian/Pacific Islander   7
Caucasian/White   57
Hispanic   4
Other   2

Institution
Doctorate-Granting   4
Master's College & University   3
Baccalaureate College   2
Community College   1

THE STUDENT EXPERIENCE IN THE ACADEMIC COMMUNITY

Many students believe: *"If students want to be dishonest, this is their business. It is an individual matter."* Furthermore, when asked about the responsibilities of students for enforcing academic integrity, one student responded: *"My only responsibility is to myself."* These beliefs are an indication that the individual conscience takes precedence over the claims of the community. This individualistic assumption can be found throughout the culture, not just among students. It is reflected in low voter turnouts for issues of social importance and exhibited in those tragic and relatively common situations where observers of a crime feel no obligation to intervene.

Today's egocentric climate encourages people to believe that they can live as they choose and has both elevated and distorted the virtue of autonomy. Without such virtues as responsibility and care, autonomy becomes moral indifference and personal disengagement. In light of this tendency toward focusing on the individual, institutions failing to nurture and enhance the relational sensitivities and skills of their students also "fail to predispose students' competence for moral behavior" (Averill, 1983).

The relationships of students and faculty are interests that emerged from several of the students' discussions: *"Levels of honesty are higher at an institution where the professors know their students, because when professors take an interest in students, students don't want to disappoint them. When you are a number, it doesn't matter."* Students often feel that they are numbers, unknown by name or distinguishing characteristics. This impersonal environment, according to some students, contributes to *"mass cheating in large lecture halls."* Anonymity also contributes to the general notion among students that *"large institutions set the stage for low integrity, while smaller institutions support and encourage high integrity."*

Morality is inherently social. Moral development requires social interactions and social relationships. There can be no sense of moral responsibility where there is no sense of personal relationship. While not all institutions of higher education can achieve the same degree of community interaction, large institutions are not exempt from the need to explore ways to do so appropriate to their settings.

Students comment frequently on the beneficial aspect of group work in classrooms and labs. For example, they believe that group assignments create a *"less competitive environment"* and encourage *"a broader exchange of ideas."* One student insists that *"all students should have classes where they work in groups."* In *Learning to be Human: A Vision for the Liberal Arts,* L.J. Averill (1983) suggested that individual work tends to be contrary to the most obvious requirements of intellectual and moral development. He explained that "moral action can take place only where the idea of responsibility makes sense; and responsibility requires that one person understands his existence to be entailed in a quite explicit and reflexive way in the existence of another — indeed, in a whole range of others" (p. 111).

Learning goes beyond the individual. Cooperative motives and reciprocal kindness supply the main structure of moral behavior. Students recognize this lack of interaction, however, and complain that *"team projects are more the exception than the rule."* Students suggest, moreover, that group work *"would curtail cheating because students would not tolerate cheating or irresponsible behavior from fellow students."* One way for institutions to contribute to the moral grounding of students is to provide learning experiences in which they can confirm and enhance their interpersonal sensitivities and skills and be accountable to one another.

According to some students, *"cheating is only cheating if I get caught."* Others feel *"if they can get away with it, it's okay."* The cynical notion that *"college is simply jumping through the necessary hoops to succeed and getting the grades any way you can"* is indeed common.

A national survey in the late 1980s found that

> cynical tendencies are growing into a consensus world view with implications for society, commerce, and the workplace. Some forty-three percent of the American populace fit the profile of the cynic, who sees selfishness and fakery at the core of human nature . . . Cynics mistrust politicians and most authority figures, regard the average person as false-faced and uncaring, and conclude that you should basically look out for yourself (Piper, Gentile & Parks, 1993, p. 2).

Institutions will have difficulty functioning effectively and resolving issues that challenge them in the face of this pervasive cynicism. As McCabe (1993) warned, cynicism about student values can become a self-fulfilling prophecy. Cynicism must be replaced in the academic community by a sense of purpose, worth, responsibility, and hope.

STUDENTS' VIEWS OF EDUCATION

Students on campuses today view the meaning and purpose of education in these ways:

"I don't think most people learn for the sake of learning, rather they learn to gain skills for better jobs."

"If education was about learning and not just making the grade, there would be no problem with cheating."

"Too much value is put on grades."
"For many students, college is simply jumping through the necessary hoops on the way to a successful career."
"Education should be about learning rather than achieving."

An essential ingredient in growth toward moral maturity is a developing sense of personal responsibility. Nothing mitigates and compromises this development in students more than the notion that an undergraduate education is primarily "preparation for later on." Students who go through their college years thinking life begins after college soon become business and professional men and women wondering when life does begin.

Twentieth-century higher education has responded quite adequately to the challenge of providing aspiring professionals with technical training, but only marginally or not at all to moral development. In *Moral Values and Higher Education,* Thompson (1991) quoted Jeffrey R. Holland, the past president of Brigham Young University:

> Although I do not wish to turn back the higher education clock to some convenient hour in the nineteenth century, I do think we might need to relearn some of the lessons taught by our forebears. Until a few decades ago . . . education was seen as a moral endeavor, not because it sought to indoctrinate but because it was a sharing of things that people held to be important . . . What we are emphasizing today, largely by default, is careerism. We seem to be turning out people who are bent upon exploiting careers for their own ends rather than upon service through their professions for the sake of society."

The Hastings Center Project on the Teaching of Ethics offered these recommendations that describe an expanded vision of the purpose of education:

> More and better courses in ethics will by no means solve the larger problems facing the university, nor will a focus on moral issues guarantee it a new purpose and vitality. Our only claim is that a higher education that does not foster, support, and implement an examination of the moral life will fail its own purpose, the needs of its students, and the welfare of society . . . We ask only that such an examination be made formal and explicit, and that sufficient imagination, energy, and resources be invested in the teaching of ethics that its importance will become manifested, both within and outside of the university (Callahan & Bok, 1980, p. 300).

With this in mind, there is concern when students comment that *"overall students don't really think about academic integrity, or talk about it either."*

Students express uneasiness about the possibility that academic institutions do not prepare them for the "real world." They complain about receiving contradictory moral messages. One student said: *"In the busi-*

ness world, the more dishonest you are the more successful you will be." Another student commented: *"You can't come to this (academic) environment and all of a sudden throw away what society believes is honest . . . you have to change society first."* When discussing the requirement in some honor codes to turn in fellow students for honor violations, an overwhelming majority of students voiced resistance and noncompliance. Some students protest that *"one of the earliest lessons we learn as a child is not to tell on others, and now we are expected to."* Others say, *"I wouldn't want the reputation of ratting."* Most students say they are not willing to put rules above friendship and state that *"it is more honorable to help your fellow students than to turn them in."*

Students realize the societal attitudes that "nice guys finish last." This is summarized by the view of one student from our focus groups: *"When you know others are cheating, it's really hard not to because you know you could do the same thing — and those who cheat have a distinct advantage."* The reasoning in no way justifies the offense, but at the very least it calls into question the arrangements that lead to it. In a system in which everyone is measured against everyone else, successes make failures, and failures make successes. This indicates a lack of reflectiveness about educational priorities, especially reliance on competitive and individualistic student learning.

CLARITY OF INSTITUTIONAL EXPECTATIONS

General consensus among students seems to be that institutional expectations exist in catalogs and handbooks; however, they are not ordinarily discussed, reviewed, or clarified. As one student explained, *"They are written in the handbook, but they are never expressed and played out for us to ponder, understand, and reflect."* Students tend to agree that the concept of academic integrity requires commitment; therefore, there must be a comprehensive understanding of clear and consistent expectations. A student offered insight, *"We are expected to know about academic integrity, but we are not necessarily told."*

Several students communicated an uncertainty about the whole notion of academic integrity. A student expressed this thoughtfully: *"Students don't know the rules. Maybe, it's not so much lack of knowledge as lack of enforcement and lack of consistency."* Another student said, *"I am unsure of expectations. What does academic dishonesty really mean?"* A third student summarized the perceptions of many students: *"There must be a policy about what cheating is, about what is allowed and what is not allowed. It cannot be assumed that students know."* Students expressed a need for definition of and insight into the institution's expectations and their responsibilities as connected to these expectations. This was expressed by one student: *"At the very least, there needs to be something that says what it means to be academically honest, along with an explanation of things not acceptable."*

One student voiced the necessity for writing all of the guidelines down: *"All of this must be written down so students will know. Rules have to be written down."* The implication is that the institution must provide both instruction and information. Added to academic integrity standards, students look to the institution to *"clear up what is cheating and not cheating"* and to teach about plagiarism. Students repeat this message over and over: *"It is the college's job to inform and teach us about academic integrity and the consequences of dishonesty."*

The institution's responsibility should be emphasized and visualized to a higher degree; this is the opinion of students who actually function with good faith efforts. Putting this in perspective, students offered wisdom: *"Everyone has the right to know what is expected. The professor for each class should provide expectation and explanation." "Faculty members have the responsibility to clarify, define, and state expectations in each syllabus." "I expect each faculty member to set the stage with specific direction."* Students imagine that they have a right to know the expectations, and that leadership with vision, direction, and strategy will be exercised in ways that generate respect for self and the quality of scholarship and honesty.

There was discussion among students at almost every institution about the value of learning and thinking (creative and critical) as opposed to memorizing. This was related to the focus on grades and to pressures to "make the grade" in order to compete for graduate and professional schools, keep scholarships, and meet expectations of parents and families. Students have different views about grades and learning. Comments and understandings were communicated in these ways:

"I want to get good grades, but I will not compromise integrity and honesty. I will do my best. If I get a B, then I did my best. This is okay."

"We need to figure out the focus: Is it grades or is it learning? This is the bottom line for cheating and academic dishonesty."

"I want to be the best student, no matter what it takes. Maybe it takes cheating on some occasions."

"People who cheat aren't learning. If you cheat, you don't get very far."

"There is too much value on grades and not enough on learning and knowledge."

"Honesty goes down as the stakes get higher, such as end of the semester, senior year, competition for graduate school."

"It is the student's responsibility to get everything possible out of class. This is the end result that really counts."

RESPONSIBILITY FOR PROMOTING ACADEMIC INTEGRITY

There was much discussion and even focus among students regarding whose job it is to set academic integrity standards and for creating a climate for student learning and personal development. A theme that was constant among students centered around their relationships with faculty and the essence of their own self-esteem and confidence. Students are eager to have the respect and trust of faculty members; they really do not want *"to let their teachers down."* Students also have pride in themselves and in their institutions and have a desire to avoid *"letting themselves down."*

Collectively and individually, students suggested that both faculty and students must *"put forth effort"* to promote academic integrity. Faculty members play an important role initially. Over time, however, it is the student's responsibility to *"get everything possible out of class"* and to visualize the concepts of performance, effort, perseverance, energy, and personal development. One student said: *"If I can think out the problem, then I don't need to cheat."* Other students described integrity as a *"personal value relevant to a successful life and career."*

How do we challenge and support students as they develop levels of reflectiveness and maturity essential for attaining high levels of knowledge and skill? Does this development include the achievement of the values important to the depth and vision of a life of worth and work? Herein lies the challenge and opportunity, along with students' hope and expectation.

Students themselves offered these suggestions: *"an academic integrity code that is communicated and celebrated," "a new version of the first year experience describing the meaning of education, learning, and academic integrity," "faculty evaluated by students on their commitments to academic integrity."* More practical suggestions included: *"standards that provide guidance and direction, sanctions that are clear and well known, and standards and sanctions posted as part of the community creed in each classroom, residence hall, and student union community."*

Students recognize their responsibility for promoting academic integrity. Without commenting necessarily on the tradition and value of honor codes, students realize that the signing of agreements, contracts, or pledges places responsibility *"on their shoulders and in their hands."* Signing a certain agreement for each test, paper, and project has merit because it promotes the understanding of expectations along with responsibility for meeting them. One student expressed clearly what many alluded to: *"The agreement or pledge defines my responsibility."*

The other strong theme among students centered around pride in accomplishment, attainment, and achievement that manifests itself in learning: attitudes of character as well as intellectual knowledge and skill. Most students are aware of orientation and first year experience programs. They believe that academic integrity based on learning might be the focus. One student expressed this thought for several: *"Isn't academic integrity the head and heart of the college experience? Why isn't it the main part of first year orientation?"*

CONCLUSIONS

Who really is responsible for promoting academic integrity? One student's vision was: *"each student personally, the peer group, the faculty, and the administration who can threaten expulsion."* Another student's vision was: *"The liberal education is worthless if students cheat. The ultimate punishment is living with the self (me)."* Students and the institution must strive for community, partnership, and mutual respect. Students see the necessity for visualizing academic integrity, defining expectations, and communicating consequences.

Finally, students will take responsibility as they have a vision for education and learning and as they view academic integrity in accordance with pride. In the words of one student, *"I am here to learn and get good grades because I work hard and study; I really do have a vision for myself and pride in my college."*

Table 2
Participating Institutions and Coordinators
Albion College . . . . Lee Williams
Appalachian State University . . . . . . Pete Wachs
Muskingham College . . . . Jerry Beavers, Mark Nelsen and Karen Smith
South Dakota School of the Mines . . Douglas K. Lange
St. John's College . . . . William Pastille
Temple University . . . . Timothy Johnson
Tompkins Cortland Community College . . . . Kathleen Damiani
University of Georgia . . . . Kenna L. Ose
University of Missouri-Rolla . . . . . William R. Wilson
Willamette University . . . . Blayne Higa and Cesie Delve Scheuermann

References

Averill, L.J. (1983). *Learning to be human: A vision for the liberal arts.* New York: Associated Faculty Press.

Callahan, D., and Bok, S. (Eds.). (1980). *Ethics teaching in higher education.* New York: The Hastings Center.

McCabe, D. (1993). *Planning for higher education.* Vol. 21.

Piper, T. R., Gentile, M. C., and Parks S. D. (1993). *Can ethics be taught?* Boston: Harvard Business School.

Thompson, D.L. (Ed). (1991). *Moral values and higher education.* New York: Brigham Young University.

THE ACADEMIC DISHONESTY OF COLLEGE STUDENTS

The Prevalence of the Problem and Effective Educational Prevention Programs

WILLIAM L. KIBLER

Research suggests that students on most, if not all, college campuses cheat on their coursework and tests. Kibler proposes that one reason why academic dishonesty persists within colleges and universities may be that institutions are treating it as a behavioral aberration rather than as an educational development issue. When cheating is discovered, most institutions address only the misbehavior, without requiring the alleged cheater to confront the developmental issues involved in deciding to use cheating as a means to achieve a goal. In failing to confront the underlying issues, colleges and universities are missing the opportunity to address the causes for breaches of academic integrity.

Academic integrity is a significant component of the philosophies and missions of many institutions of higher education (Stovall, 1989). Universities and colleges, regardless of their constitution, are responsible for providing an environment conducive to learning and excellence (Raffetto, 1985).

ACADEMIC DISHONESTY DEFINED

One of the most significant problems associated with a literature review of academic dishonesty issues is the absence of a generally accepted definition of the subject. Academic dishonesty usually refers to forms of cheating and plagiarism that result in students giving or receiving unauthorized assistance in an academic exercise or receiving credit for work that is not their own (Kibler, Nuss, Paterson & Pavela, 1988).

A variety of student behaviors exists that may constitute academic dishonesty. Hetherington and Feldman (1964) categorized cheating as: a) individualistic-opportunistic, unplanned and impulsive; b) individualistic-planned, involving elements of foresight and activity before an actual test situation; c) social-active, involving two or more people who instigate cheating; and d) social-passive, two or more people allowing others to copy from them.

Most incidents of academic dishonesty fit traditional patterns: taking an exam for another student; altering or forging an official document; paying someone else to write a paper to submit as one's own work; arranging to give or receive answers by use of signals; getting questions and answers from someone who has taken the exam; copying with or without the other person's knowledge; completing assignments for someone; plagiarizing; and padding items on a bibliography.

Other unethical practices include: obtaining a copy of a test, using unauthorized notes, working together with other students on assignments when it is not allowed, using "crib sheets," turning in stolen exams as tests taken in class, changing grades and answers, and using an instructor's manual (Barnett & Dalton, 1981; Nuss, 1984; Raffetto, 1985; Singhal & Johnson, 1983).

Pavela (1978) proposed the following definitions:

■ Cheating — intentionally using or attempting to use unauthorized materials, information, or study aids in any academic exercise. The term *academic exercise* includes all forms of work submitted for credit or hours.

■ Fabrication — intentional and unauthorized falsification or invention of any information or citation in an academic exercise.

■ Facilitating Academic Dishonesty — intentionally or knowingly helping or attempting to help another to violate a provision of the institutional code of academic integrity.

■ Plagiarism — the deliberate adoption or reproduction of ideas or words or statements of another person as one's own without acknowledgment (p. 68).

CONTEMPORARY CONTEXT

American higher education traditionally has reviewed its role as encompassing more than just the acquisition of knowledge and the development of intellectual competence. Its goals generally have been described as helping students expand their knowledge and intellectual powers; enhancing students' moral, religious, and emotional interests and sensibilities; and improving their performance in citizenship, work, family life, consumer choice, health, and other practical matters (Bowen, 1980).

During the last 25 years, student development theorists have agreed that the collegiate experience should enable students to mature and grow along several dimensions. Chickering (1969) proposed that these dimensions include: developing intellectual competence; learning to manage emotions; developing and establishing autonomy; establishing identity; developing interpersonal relations; developing a sense of purpose; and developing integrity. The manner in which colleges and universities have attempted to accomplish these goals and individuals responsible have changed over the course of history (Sandeen, 1985).

Throughout the 1980s, national attention was focused on how well higher education accomplished its goals. Various reports [Study Group on the Condition of Excellence in American Higher Education (1984), Project on Redefining the Meaning and Purpose of the Baccalaureate Degrees (1985) and the Newman Report (1985)] raised questions about the quality of baccalaureate programs. These reports documented concern for the general condition of undergraduate programs and urged the academic community to systemically encourage integrity and coherence in undergraduate programs. Evidence indicates that many college graduates are unable to perform fundamental tasks associated with effective communication, logical problem solving, persuasive argument, and critical analysis of data (Kibler, et al., 1988).

Serious questions have also been raised about the ability of today's college students to understand and appreciate complex societal problems, many of which have an ethical component (Hesburgh, 1985). More recently, the American College Personnel Association (1994) published a report titled *The Student Learning Imperative* and the National Association for Student Personnel Administrators (1994) published a report titled *Reasonable Expectations*. Both these reports outline the challenges ahead for institutions, faculty, and students in addressing learning and development needs of college students.

The questions and challenges raised by these reports are evidence that higher education is facing a crisis in fulfilling its most fundamental purposes. The trust and subsequent support American higher education has traditionally relied upon may be limited as its constituents — students, parents, legislators, alumni, and citizens — question its value. Reports of academic dishonesty and cheating contribute to this erosion of confidence and public support (Kibler et al., 1988).

The Carnegie Foundation for the Advancement of Teaching conducted a comprehensive national study on campus community (Boyer, 1990). This report identified six principles that characterize campus community. The first principle identified was: a college or university is an educationally purposeful community, a place where faculty and students share academic goals and work together to strengthen teaching and learning on campus.

Academic dishonesty presents a serious threat to maintaining an educationally purposeful community by undermining the foundation of an institution's integrity. Failure to provide and enforce adequate penalties in effect communicates approval to students, especially those who enter college with cheating patterns already in place. As a result, the value a college or university places on academic integrity is perceived as very low. Institutions cannot afford to ignore academic dishonesty (Stovall, 1989).

EXTENT OF THE PROBLEM

Cheating behaviors can be traced in history through thousands of years. Brickman (1961) reported that during the civil service examinations in ancient China, tests were given in individual cubicles to prevent examinees from looking at the test papers of others, that examinees were searched for notes before they entered the cubicles, and that the death penalty was in effect for both examinees and examiners if anyone was found guilty of cheating. Despite such methods, cheating still occurred.

Cheating is not confined to colleges and universities. In a study by Schab (1969), approximately 24 percent of the girls and 20 percent of the boys admitted that they began cheating in the first grade; 17 percent of the girls and 15 percent of the boys began in the eighth grade; and 13 percent of the girls and 9 percent of the boys began in the seventh grade. A recent survey of over 3,000 high achievers in high school conducted by Who's Who Among American High School Students (1994) showed that most of the nation's top high school students cheat in school. Nearly 80 percent of students with an A or B average surveyed said they have cheated on their schoolwork. Of those who cheated, 93 percent said they have never been caught. Academic dishonesty is also not unique to undergraduate students. Zastrow (1970) provided evidence of a 40 percent incidence of cheating among graduate students.

While there is debate about whether acts of academic dishonesty in higher education have increased, it is clear that the problem on most campuses is significant (Gehring, Nuss & Pavela, 1986). One of the last reports issued by the Carnegie Council on Policy Studies in Higher Education (1979), *Fair Practices in Higher Education*, amounted to an indictment of both students and colleges for what the council viewed as a rise in unethical conduct, from classroom cheating to false advertising by institutions and abuse of student aid. The report cited anonymous surveys at several campuses in which 30-40 percent of students confessed to cheating at least once. Carnegie's own surveys found that from 1969 to 1976, the percentage of students who responded that "some forms of cheating are necessary to get what I want" varied from 7.5 to 8.8 percent. At research universities, the percentage more than doubled during this period from 4.5 to 9.8 percent.

Researchers have studied and documented academic dishonesty on American college campuses for over 50 years. Studies report that anywhere from 13 percent to 95 percent of college students engage in some form of academic dishonesty (Collison, 1990; Eve & Bromley, 1981; Haines, 1986; Harp & Taietz, 1966; Jendrek, 1989; Leming, 1980; Liska, 1978; Tittle & Rowe, 1974). McCabe and Trevino (1993) observed that the definition of academic dishonesty, the data collection methods employed, and other variables affect the results of these studies. During this time, higher education appears to have experienced a gradual increase in academic dishonesty. A study by Drake (1941) found that 23 percent of college students cheated. Goldsen (1960) reported that 38 percent of students admitted cheating in an earlier study and that figure increased to 49 percent in a similar study done in 1960. Since that time studies have reported 50-75 percent of students involved in cheating (Ludeman, 1988; Pavela, 1981). Furthermore, several campuses have reported studies in which over 75 percent of students surveyed admitted to engaging in some form of academic dishonesty (Baird, 1980).

McCabe (McCabe & Trevino, 1993) surveyed over 6,000 students at 31 selective colleges and universities across the country. More than 67 percent of the students responding reported that they had engaged in cheating while in college, and over 40 percent admitted to cheating on exams. His study, conducted in 1991, focused on small to medium size colleges, which were largely residential in nature.

McCabe (McCabe & Trevino, 1993) also found that students at larger universities are much more likely to engage in academic dishonesty, particularly repeated acts of the most serious forms of dishonesty than those at smaller schools. He studied the extent of self-reported cheating by 1,800 students at nine medium to large state universities that were surveyed in 1962 by Bowers (1964). McCabe found that the level of cheating increased significantly over the last 30 years. For example, the number of students admitting to copying from another on an exam went from 26 percent in 1962 to 52 percent in 1993. In the same study, McCabe found that 38 percent of the students surveyed at large state universities admitted to some form of cheating on three or more occasions. In contrast to Bower's 1962 data, McCabe found that women reported levels of cheating comparable to men.

According to Gehring et al. (1986), such evidence of widespread academic dishonesty poses a substantial threat to the higher educational enterprise in at least four ways:

- A campus climate that appears to be tolerant of academic dishonesty may have the perverse effect of encouraging students who did not cheat in secondary school to adopt such a practice in college and throughout their lives. Such an outcome is the antithesis of what the college and university experience is designed to accomplish.
- Apparent faculty indifference to academic dishonesty communicates to students that the values of integrity and honesty are not sufficiently important to justify any serious effort to enforce them. This is a potentially devastating moral example for a generation of students which Yankelovich (1981) described as lacking clearly defined goals and longing for an ethic of commitment.
- Many students are justifiably outraged when faculty and staff members appear to ignore obvious cases of cheating or plagiarism. Such feelings, should they become prevalent, have the potential to damage any sense of community on campus and alienate some of the very best students from the institution.
- Academic dishonesty deceives those who may eventually depend upon the knowledge and integrity of our graduates. For example, a

study in the *Journal of Medical Education* found a positive correlation between cheating in medical school and cheating in clinical patient care by young physicians (Sierles, Hendricks & Circle, 1980).

EFFECTIVE EDUCATIONAL INTERVENTION

Pavela (1981) stated that the increased willingness of students to engage in dishonest or unethical behaviors has continued in part due to vague policies and procedures, laxity in proctoring exams, and lenient penalties. The academic community does not discuss the value it places on integrity (Nuss, 1984). In Nuss' study, approximately one-half of the faculty indicated that they never or rarely discuss university policies or their own requirements pertaining to academic dishonesty. Nuss concluded that without sufficient opportunities for discussion, it is difficult, if not impossible, for new generations of college students to become aware of the values associated with effective scholarship.

Kibler et al. (1988) argued that even though the precise causes of academic dishonesty were unclear and the extent of the problem was unknown, colleges and universities needed to initiate systematic and conscientious efforts to help students appreciate the fundamental values associated with effective scholarship and academic integrity. They further stated that it is incumbent upon students, faculty, and administrators to design ways to help students respond to ethical dilemmas. While each campus has its own unique mission and value system or ethos, it is safe to conclude that all institutions agree on the necessity for academic integrity. Nuss (1981) stated that the student development theoretical framework provides guidance for the design of proposed approaches to the problem of academic dishonesty.

Nuss (1981) argued that the effectiveness of the actions that colleges and universities take to enhance academic integrity can be improved if they are planned within the context of moral development theory. The Carnegie Council (1979) and others have recommended specific steps colleges and universities should take (Gehring et al., 1986; Kibler et al, 1988; Levine, 1980; Pavela, 1981). Several of these steps were discussed by Nuss within the context of the development framework in Kibler et al. (1988). These included the importance of a clearly written policy; opportunities for discussion and dialogue; equitable adjudication procedures; the role of sanctions; and the importance of instructional settings. These steps are discussed in summary form below and are endorsed by others in this monograph:

■ *Clearly written policy.* The student development literature emphasizes the important role the environment plays in fostering development. Clearly communicating the community's expectations for academic integrity is one important way for the environment to foster student development. Institutional policies and expectations should include: definitions of academic dishonesty; examples of behaviors that constitute infractions; a description of the process followed when alleged violations occur; and a description of the sanctions usually imposed.

■ *Opportunities for discussion and dialogue.* The literature indicates that students are at different places developmentally and that development is facilitated by opportunities to role play and confront different social and moral perspectives. Frequent discussions about academic integrity provide the institution with an opportunity to communicate the value it places on integrity relative to other values such as achievement and competition. With this approach, students have the opportunity to seek clarification or elaboration and could become familiar with the way different disciplines or professions view integrity and ethical questions. The discussions may help students avoid unintentional violations as a result of ignorance or misunderstanding.

■ *Equitable adjudication procedures.* Equitable procedures for resolving cases of alleged academic dishonesty should be considered within the context of the theoretical framework. The procedures should be compatible with the institutional mission and the needs of the campus community and should ensure due process for all parties. Campus procedures should provide the student with the opportunity to confront the ethical implications of their behavior, gain a better understanding of the roles and the responsibilities of students and faculty within the academic community, develop an appreciation of the values associated with effective scholarship, and gain exposure to forms of moral reasoning they can comprehend and that are likely to stimulate their development.

■ *Role of sanctions.* Pavela (1981) argued effectively against the practice of simply giving a student a failing grade for academic dishonesty for several reasons. The practice does not serve as a deterrent to students already in jeopardy of failing, and it misleads other schools to which the student may apply. Most important, the practice deprives the student of an adequate opportunity to confront the ethical implications of the behavior. Consistently applied sanctions represent the essence of challenge and support.

■ *Instructional settings.* To facilitate the moral development of students, the actions of the academic community must be consistent with its published statements and policies. Conditions that facilitate academic dishonesty and fail to insist that faculty members demonstrate high ethical standards communicate a mixed message to students and create an environment which is not conducive to student development.

INSTITUTIONAL APPROACHES TO PREVENTING CHEATING

College administrators seem unsure of how to approach the problem. Kibler (1994) discovered, after conducting a study of nearly 200 colleges and universities across the country in 1991, that on many campuses little is being done to prevent or deal effectively with cheating. Following is a summary of some disturbing results of the research:

■ *Unavailability of data:* Nearly one-half of the institutions could not report the number of cases of cheating handled on their campus over the previous three academic years because they had not kept records.

■ *Lack of honor codes:* Only 27 percent of the institutions had honor codes. Fewer than half of those institutions had implemented the elements to make them "working honor codes," such as requiring students to sign a pledge stating they would not cheat; mandating that students report offenders; and administering unproctored exams.

■ *Inadequate involvement of faculty members and students:* Only two-thirds of the institutions reported that faculty members were involved in developing and enforcing standards, and only one-third said that students were involved.

■ *Lack of coordination:* Two-thirds of the institutions reported that no office or person was responsible for coordinating efforts to prevent cheating or to promote academic integrity.

■ *Lack of training:* Fewer than half of the institutions offered any kind of training to faculty members or teaching assistants on how to deal with academic dishonesty. Almost 70 percent of the individuals responsible for determining sanctions for cheating had no training in student development, making it unlikely that the developmental level of the student, such as his or her decision-making skills or ability to relate to moral reasoning and behavior, was considered and less likely

that sanctions such as required educational seminars were used.
- ■ *Lack of educational programs:* Only 3 percent (six institutions) required students who were caught cheating to participate in some educational program designed to help them reconsider their behavior. The most prevalent sanctions were just to fail the student on the assignment or in the course.

CONCLUSIONS

Unfortunately, there is no quick fix, no single or simple solution to the problem of student cheating. Adopting an honor code and widely publicizing it is not enough. Institutions must adopt a comprehensive approach involving the entire institution — students, faculty members, and administrators.

One possible solution is built on the concept that the most effective way to prevent cheating is to actively promote academic integrity, while effectively confronting those who cheat. Included in these confrontations should be sanctions that respond to the behavior as well as educational programs or seminars that address developmental issues.

The first step is for institutions to establish an ethos that defines, promotes, and reveres academic integrity. The creation of such an ethos can start with honor codes, codes of conduct, and other official declarations that clarify three important issues regarding academic integrity: expectation of student honesty; punishment for those who do cheat; and the potential for long-term negative results of cheating. Institutions must help students understand the value of integrity and the achievement of grades based on honest accomplishment. Another important responsibility of institutions is to help students understand that cheating behaviors established in college are very likely to continue into their professional careers.

After setting its standards, the institution then must use all the tools it has to communicate its position on academic integrity and its intention not to tolerate dishonesty: direct correspondence to faculty members and students; mandated discussions about cheating during orientation meetings for students and faculty members, as well as during individual classes at the beginning of semesters; printed materials such as handbooks; and the campus news media.

Faculty members are the most critical element in ensuring the success of any campus-wide effort to promote academic integrity. They should reflect, communicate, and enforce the institution's values. They should also be involved in developing and implementing whatever system the institution creates; their participation will give them a sense of personal commitment to and ownership of the system.

Many faculty members refuse to address the problem of academic dishonesty because they feel the rules are too complicated and the procedures for enforcing them too time-consuming. Others try to minimize the problem for fear that it may reflect badly on their ability to teach. Young faculty members, in particular, may ignore cheating because it might reveal that they lack the skills or experience to avert it. Still others do not like to report cheating because they do not want to be branded as "zealots" or "troublemakers" by colleagues or students. The institution must help train faculty members in ways to prevent cheating and in how to create a classroom atmosphere in which honesty is clearly the expected standard.

It is also essential that students be involved in developing and carrying out systems to promote academic integrity. Failure to involve students creates an "us vs. them" atmosphere that tends to promote cheating. Students can serve on honor or disciplinary boards and on review committees that assess how well an institution's process for assuring academic integrity is working.

Finally, an institution must coordinate its efforts to ensure that all the elements of its system are implemented. One office should be responsible for monitoring relevant data, assessing the effectiveness of policies and procedures, coordinating communication efforts, and coordinating training programs on academic dishonesty and ways to prevent it.

Besides acting to create an ethos of academic integrity, institutions must develop policies that deal effectively with students who still choose to cheat. Those policies should include:

■ *Appropriate sanctions.* These might include a notation concerning academic dishonesty on a transcript, required counseling, and required attendance at a class or seminar on academic integrity.

■ *A required educational program for offenders.* Such a program should include discussion of what cheating is and why it is unacceptable. It should also include education in moral development to help students understand the relationship between moral reasoning and behavior. By using discussions, case studies, and role-playing exercises, students can be helped in responding to ethical dilemmas. Finally, the program should include training in academic skills to help students gain confidence in their abilities to succeed in the classroom without cheating.

■ *Testing policies that emphasize prevention of cheating.* These could include procedures that protect the security of tests before they are administered; proctoring services; assigned seating and use of different versions of the same test during exams; and guidelines for making writing assignments that limit opportunities for plagiarism.

■ *Methods of reporting cheating that are unintimidating.* These methods could include, for example, anonymity for persons who report cheating.

Faculty members and administrators can no longer ignore their responsibilities to promote academic integrity. They must help students develop the values they need to deal effectively with the moral and ethical dilemmas facing them.

Clearly communicating an institution's expectations for academic honesty is an important way to foster students' development. Frequent discussions about integrity enable academics to communicate the value they place on integrity relative to other values such as achievement and competition. When cheating does occur, campus procedures should make students confront the ethical implications of their behavior, expose them to discussion of moral reasoning, and help them understand that effective learning depends on honesty, respect, rigor, and fairness.

References

American College Personnel Association (1994). *Student learning imperative: Implications for student affairs.* Washington, D.C.: author.

Baird, J.S. (1980). Current trends in college cheating. *Psychology in the Schools, 17,* 515-522.

Barnett, D.C., and Dalton, J.C. (1981). Why college students cheat. *Journal of College Student Personnel, 22,* 545-551.

Bowen, H.R. (1980). *Investment in learning: The individual and social value of American higher education.* San Francisco: Jossey-Bass, Inc.

Bowers, W.J. (1964). *Student dishonesty and its control in college.* New York: Bureau of Applied Social Research, Columbia University.

Boyer, E. (1990). *Campus life: In search of community.* Princeton, N.J.: The Carnegie Foundation for the Advancement of Teaching.

Brickman, W.W. (1961). Ethics, examinations and education. *School and Society, 89,* 412-415.

Carnegie Council on Policy Studies in Higher Education. (1979). *Fair practices in higher education: Rights and responsibilities in a period of intensified competition for enrollment.* San Francisco: Jossey-Bass, Inc.

Chickering, A. (1969). *Education and identity.* San Francisco: Jossey-Bass, Inc.

Collison, M. (1990, January 17). Apparent rise in students' cheating has college official worried. *The Chronicle of Higher Education,* p. A33.

Drake, C.A. (1941). Why students cheat. *Journal of Higher Education, 12,* 418-420.

Eve, R.A., and Bromley, D.G. (1981). Scholastic dishonesty among college undergraduates: Parallel tests of two sociological explanations. *Youth and Society, 13,* 3-22.

Gehring, D., Nuss, E.M., and Pavela, G. (1986). *Issues and perspectives on academic integrity.* Columbus, OH: National Association of Student Personnel Administrators.

Goldsen, R.K. (1960). *What college students think.* Princeton, N.J.: Von Nostrand.

Haines, V.J. (1986). College cheating: Immaturity, lack of commitment and the neutralizing attitude. *Research in Higher Education, 25,* 342-354.

Harp, J., and Taietz, P. (1966). Academic integrity and social structure: A study of cheating among college students. *Social Problems, 13,* 365-373.

Hesburgh, T. M. (1985). The role of the academy in the nuclear age. In J.B. Bennett & J.W. Peltason (Eds.). *Contemporary issues in higher education.* New York: Macmillan Publishers.

Hetherington, E.M., and Feldman S.E. (1964). College cheating as a function of subject and situational variables. *Journal of Educational Psychology, 55,* 212-218.

Jendrek, M.P. (1989). Faculty reaction to academic dishonesty. *Journal of College Student Development, 30,* 401-406.

Kibler, W.L. (1994). Addressing academic dishonesty: What institutions of higher education are doing and not doing? *NASPA Journal, 31,* 92-101.

Kibler, W.L., Nuss, E.M., Paterson, B.G., and Pavela, G. (1988). *Academic integrity and student development: Legal issues, policy perspectives.* Asheville, N.C.: College Administration Publications.

Leming, J.S. (1980). Cheating behavior, subject variables, and components of the internal-external scale under high and low risk conditions. *Journal of Educational Research, 74,* 83-87.

Levine, A. (1980). *When dreams and heroes died: A portrait of today's college student.* San Francisco: Jossey-Bass, Inc.

Liska, A. (1978). Deviant involvement, associations and attitudes: Specifying the underlying causal structures. *Sociology and Social Research, 63,* 73 - 88.

Ludeman, R.B. (1988). A survey of academic integrity practices in U.S. higher education. *Journal of College Student Development, 29* (2), 172-173.

McCabe, D.L. (1992). The influence of situational ethics on cheating among college students. *Sociological Inquiry, 63* (3), 365-374.

McCabe, D.L., and Trevino, L.K. (1993). Academic dishonesty: Honor codes and other contextual influences. *Journal of Higher Education, 64* (5), 522-538.

National Association of Student Personnel Administrators. (1994). *Reasonable expectations.* Washington, D.C.: author.

Newman, F. (1985). *Higher education and the American resurgence.* Princeton, N.J.: The Carnegie Foundation for the Advancement of Teaching.

Nuss, E.M. (1981). Undergraduate moral development and academic dishonesty (Doctoral dissertation, University of Maryland, 1981) *Dissertation Abstracts International, 42,* 3463A.

Nuss, E.M. (1984). Academic integrity: Comparing faculty and student attitudes. *Improving College and University Teaching, 32*(3), 140-144.

Pavela, G. (1978). Judicial review of academic decision making after Horowitz. *School Law Journal, 55*(8), 55-75.

Pavela, G. (1981, February 9). Cheating on campus. Who's really to blame? *The Chronicle of Higher Education,* p. 64.

Project on Redefining the Meaning and Purpose of the Baccalaureate Degrees. (1985). *Integrity in the college curriculum: A report to the academic community.* Washington, D.C.: Association of American Colleges.

Raffetto, W.G. (1985). The cheat. *Community and Junior College Journal, 56* (2), 26-27.

Sandeen, C.A. (1985). The legacy of values education in college student personnel work. In J. Dalton (Ed.), *Promoting values development in college students.* Washington, D.C.: National Association of Student Personnel Administrators.

Schab, F. (1969). Cheating in high school. *Journal of the National Association of Women Deans and Counselors, 33,* 39-42.

Sierles, F., Hendricks, I., and Circle, S. (1980). Cheating in medical school. *Journal of Medical Education, 55,* 124-125.

Singhal, A.C., and Johnson, P. (1983). How to halt student dishonesty. *College Student Journal, 17* (1), 13-19.

Stovall, J.L. (1989). Academic integrity: A joint responsibility of administrators, faculty and students. *Carolina View, 4,* 36-38.

Study Group on the Condition of Excellence in American Higher Education. (1984). *Involvement in learning: Realizing the potential of American higher education.* Washington, D.C.: National Institute of Education.

Tittle, C.R., and Rowe, A.R. (1974). Fear and the student cheater. *Change, 6*(3), 47-48.

Who's Who Among American High School Students. (1994). *Twenty-fifth annual survey of high achievers.* Lake Forest, Ill.: Educational Communications, Inc.

Yankelovich, D. (1981). *New rules, searching for self-fulfillment in a world turned upside down.* New York: Random House.

Zastrow, C.H. (1970). Cheating among college graduate students. *Journal of Educational Research, 64,* 157-160.

4

THE CLASSROOM ENVIRONMENT AND ACADEMIC INTEGRITY

A Behavioral Science Perspective

BERNARD E. WHITLEY, JR.
MARY E. KITE

Kibler suggested a number of campus-based strategies that begin to address academic integrity issues at institutions of higher education. In this chapter, Whitley and Kite continue this discussion by focusing on the classroom environment from a behavioral science perspective.

The prevalence of academic dishonesty may surprise some faculty. Recent surveys suggest that as many as 95 percent of college students have engaged in at least one cheating incident during their academic careers (Davis, Grover, Becker & McGregor, 1992; McCabe & Trevino, 1993; see also Kibler, Chapter 3). Although the actual percentage of students who cheat is unknown, few experienced instructors would doubt that cheating is rampant in higher education institutions. The sheer number of students who engage in this behavior certainly suggests that effective solutions to this problem are long overdue.

Researchers who study academic dishonesty have most often considered the prevalence of cheating (Maramark & Maline, 1993), individual differences in the propensity to cheat (Eisenberger, 1992; Haines, Diekhoff, LaBeff & Clark, 1986), or institutional factors that contribute to cheating (May & Loyd, 1993). Unfortunately, this work offers little insight as to why and when students cheat. Such factors as the stress of the academic environment and competition are noted as likely causes (Maramark & Maline, 1993), but theoretical discussions of why and how those factors operate to produce academic dishonesty are lacking. A theoretical focus, grounded in behavioral science research, would be beneficial in that researchers could identify causes of cheating and, based on those causes, suggest better and more effective ways to lower the incidence of academic dishonesty. By taking a behavioral science perspective, we offer a framework for understanding students' academic dishonesty. In doing so, we discuss three themes: students' lack of knowledge of inappropriate behavior, their motivation to perform inappropriate behavior, and situational constraints on inappropriate behavior. Our perspective focuses on factors that are under the instructor's control, such as providing appropriate information or effectively monitoring student behavior, rather than factors that might influence academic dishonesty but are outside the instructor's control, such as students' attitudes and personalities. We conclude with discussions of how to handle cheating and of students' perceptions of whether cheating is worth the risk of being caught.

AWARENESS OF INAPPROPRIATE BEHAVIOR

To avoid engaging in inappropriate behaviors, students must first know the behaviors to avoid. Although students can be expected to clearly understand that some forms of academic dishonesty, such as cheating on tests, are inappropriate, other forms, such as unauthorized cooperation between students or unauthorized help from others on homework assignments and term papers, may need to be defined for each course, and perhaps for each assignment (Cole, 1995). Such understanding is related to cheating: In a survey of over 6,000 college students, McCabe and Trevino (1993) found that students who better understood institutional policies on academic dishonesty were less likely to cheat. In addition, even when students know that a behavior is wrong, they may engage in it inadvertently because although they know the dictionary definition of the behavior, they cannot identify it in practice. For example, Roig and Hill (1995) found that as many as two-thirds of the students they surveyed could not correctly identify some forms of plagiarism when comparing a plagiarized passage with the original.

To alleviate the problem of students' lack of knowledge of behaviors to avoid, instructors should clearly delineate the kinds of behaviors that are unacceptable on tests, out-of-class assignments, and term papers. Roig and Hill's work suggested that instructors should take special care in defining plagiarism, especially behaviors the academic community may define as plagiarism but are not included in its dictionary definition. For example, self-plagiarism in the form of submitting the same term paper for multiple courses is forbidden in most academic institutions but is not part of the dictionary definition of plagiarism. Instructors should explain these policies both orally and in writing (ideally in the course syllabus) to facilitate students' complete understanding. Wilhoit (1994) suggested that the explanation include clear definitions of inappropriate behaviors and clear guidelines for what constitutes proper collaboration among students. He also suggested that the guidelines be illustrated with hypothetical cases. These case studies can be provided in writing as a focus for discussing academic dishonesty with students. Cole (1995) provided some examples of cases that can be used in discussions of plagiarism.

MOTIVATION TO CHEAT

Theory and research in social psychology suggest that there are several aspects of students' social environments that can affect their motivation to cheat. These factors include a desire to achieve at a level beyond one's current ability, a desire to maintain a feeling of fairness in instructor-student relationships, and a desire to maintain a sense of control over the events that affect one's life. To the extent that instructors can control the situational factors that influence these motives, they may be able to reduce the frequency of cheating.

Success as a Motive for Cheating
Students frequently report that they cheat in order to do better than they would by study or effort alone. For example, Davis and Ludvigson (1995) reported that 29 percent of the students in their survey who admitted to cheating also said that they studied for the tests they cheated on but wanted

to enhance their scores. Students often attribute this desire to "overachieve" to factors such as pressure from parents, fear of a competitive job market, or a need to impress graduate school admissions committees (Lipson & McGavern, 1993). Although it is easy to dismiss such excuses as rationalizations that students engage in to avoid accepting responsibility for their actions (McCabe, 1992), many students may indeed perceive themselves to be under such pressures (Fass, 1990) so as to justify their actions. Other students may have more mercenary motives, as illustrated by the comment one student wrote in response to a question in a survey conducted by the first author: "Anything worth having is worth cheating for."

Instructors can forestall student attempts to achieve beyond their abilities and the temptations to cheat that might accompany those attempts by taking steps to ensure that the students who enroll in their classes have the knowledge and skills required to succeed in it. The traditional means of doing this is by establishing course prerequisites. It is important, however, to review prerequisite courses and their content periodically to ensure that students are getting the appropriate background. It is also important to enforce prerequisites. Not all computerized registration systems check that students have completed all prerequisites, so the instructor should verify students' qualifications. Instructors can also administer pretests to ensure that students can do the required work, although such pretests should be administered early enough in the course that students can change their registration if they do not do well on them. Similarly, students should be given opportunities to complete some course assignments early in the term, so they can gauge whether they are sufficiently prepared for the course, and so those who are not can withdraw.

McKeachie (1994) suggested that it can also be useful to provide students with multiple opportunities to meet course goals; grading solely on the basis of one or two exams might place undue stress on students. Similarly, these opportunities should take a variety of forms. Some students do better on multiple-choice test questions, others on short answer or essay questions, and others on reports and term papers. Knowing that they have the opportunity to show their strong points will also reduce stress on students.

Fairness as a Motive for Cheating

Fass (1990) noted that "students frequently report that cheating increases when students perceive tests or grading procedures to be unfair" (p. 180). This suggestion that cheating may stem in part from students' perceptions of unfairness is consistent with the principles of equity theory (Mowday,

1991), which addresses the issues of fairness and the ways in which people attempt to rectify instances of perceived unfairness. The theory views fairness in terms of a social exchange: the rewards one receives from an endeavor should be proportional to the resources and effort one puts into the endeavor. Conversely, unfairness or inequity exists when one's rewards are disproportionate to one's inputs. Although the theory holds that both over- and under-reward produce feelings of inequity, it is under-reward that has been most studied, and it is in that sense that the term *inequity* is used here.

Inequity is an aversive state, so people are motivated to reduce it by establishing equitable relationships. Equity theory proposes several mechanisms for reducing feelings of inequity, the most studied of which is reducing one's inputs to match one's rewards (Mowday, 1991). For example, workers who believe that they are underpaid often reduce their productivity to a level that they feel is consistent with the rewards they receive. One can also act to increase one's own outcomes, an action that can sometimes take the form of dishonest behavior. For example, industrial psychologists have found that when workers feel that they are underpaid, they sometimes resort to stealing from their employers as a means of increasing their rewards to levels that they see as fair. Greenberg (1990) found that in one factory the employee theft rate rose from 3 percent prior to a temporary pay cut to 8 percent during the pay cut period, returning to 3 percent after the former pay levels were restored. A similar factory operated by the same company that did not experience a pay cut had an employee theft rate of 3 percent throughout this time period.

College students can also resort to dishonest behavior to relieve feelings of inequity. For example, DeMore, Fisher, and Baron (1988) found that students who felt unfairly treated by their university were more likely to admit to having vandalized university facilities, and Greenberg (1993) found that college students were more likely to steal from an experimenter who paid them less than they were promised than from an experimenter who made the promised payment.

Feelings of inequity may also be a cause of college students' academic dishonesty: in response to an open-ended question about why they would allow other students access to their answers during exams, Davis, Grover, Becker, and McGregor (1992) found that several of their respondents mentioned equity-related issues, such as "I knew they studied and knew the material, but test taking was really difficult" (p. 17). College students therefore appear to view cheating as a legitimate response to what they perceive to be unfair treatment by a professor, a view that is congruent with the tenets of equity theory and with the results of research on responses to inequity (see also McKeachie, 1994). Consequently, instructors may be able to reduce students' motivation to cheat by ensuring that an atmosphere of fairness prevails in their classrooms.

Perceived fairness can be enhanced by ensuring that assignments and test questions are appropriate to the level and goals of the course, that students are given the skills and information required to meet performance standards, and that they have enough time on assignments and tests so they can do well. Instructors can also enhance the perceived fairness of assignments, policies, and procedures by explaining the reasons for them and the ways in which they contribute to the goals of the course. Greenberg (1990, 1993) found that both factory workers and college students were less likely to engage in dishonest behaviors when apparently unfair policies were fully explained to them.

Control as a Motive for Cheating
People raised in the European-American cultural milieu have a very strong need to feel in control of the factors that affect their lives; as a result, they have a strong motivation to assert that control when they feel that it is threatened (Brehm & Brehm, 1981; Fiske & Taylor, 1991). Therefore, if students believe that they have little control over their academic outcomes, they might resort to cheating as a means of asserting such control. For example, if they believe that their efforts have no effect on their grades or that their instructors are not responsive to their needs and concerns, they might view cheating as one way of controlling the grades they get or of succeeding despite their instructors' apparent lack of concern.

The research conducted by DeMore et al. (1988) and Greenberg (1993) also suggested that the effect of the equity of an assignment might be moderated by perceptions of the professor. DeMore et al. (1988) found that differences in perceptions of control over the sources of inequity were related to differences in response to perceived inequity: the level of vandalism reported by students who were low in both perceived equity and perceived control was higher than that of other students. In a similar vein, Greenberg (1993) found responses to inequity depended on the experimenter's degree of interpersonal sensitivity: students who were treated equitably stole little regardless of the experimenter's level of sensitivity, but inequitably treated students stole less from an experimenter who was sympathetic to their plight than to one who was unsympathetic.

Instructors can enhance students' perceptions of control over their academic outcomes by being responsive to their needs and concerns. For example, one can allow students to appeal grades on tests and assignments and make appropriate grade changes if the appeal is well-grounded or fully explain the reasons for not granting the appeal. Instructors can also be flexible in enforcing their policies, making exceptions when students' circumstances justify them. Finally, students may feel that they have more control over their academic outcomes when grading is criterion referenced rather than norm referenced (Gronlund, 1993). In norm-referenced grading (grading "on the curve"), each student's grade is determined by his or her standing relative to all other students in the class; consequently, a grade is determined not only by a student's own level of performance but also by the performance of all other students, a factor outside any one student's control. In criterion-referenced grading, students are evaluated against absolute standards of performance (e.g., A = 90 percent or higher), so that the grade depends only on the students' performance level, which they may see as more controllable than others' performance.

CONSTRAINTS ON BEHAVIOR

Even as some factors motivate people to perform a behavior such as cheating, other factors can constrain the performance of the behavior. Such constraining factors can counteract or reduce the influence of the motivational factors. Because potential dispositional and social constraints on cheating are not under the control of the instructor and so cannot be used as part of a classroom management program, we will touch on them only briefly. We will discuss two potential situational constraints more fully.

Dispositional and Social Norm Constraints

Behavioral scientists use the term *dispositions* to refer to the internal (as opposed to situational) factors that influence behavior. Dispositions include such factors as personality characteristics, attitudes, and values. As McCabe and Trevino (1993) have noted, much of the research on cheating has focused on the roles of dispositional factors, which are clearly related to cheating and other forms of academic dishonesty. Beck and Ajzen (1991), for example, found that students' personal moral standards assessed during one semester predicted whether they cheated on a test or lied to delay turning in an assignment during the following semester, even after controlling for their having cheated or lied in the past. In Chapter 1, Dalton discusses some of these dispositional factors in more detail.

Social norms are people's perceptions of the rules that govern their behavior in a given situation, based on what they believe is expected of them by people whose opinions they value. Beck and Ajzen (1991) found that students' norms regarding academic dishonesty were correlated with their having cheated, and McCabe and Trevino (1993) found that in colleges and universities that had honor codes, pressure from fellow students not to cheat was correlated with students' resistance to cheating. McKeachie (1994) also noted that norms against cheating are most likely to develop in small classes or when large lecture classes also meet in smaller discussion or laboratory sections.

Situational Factors
Faculty want to believe the best of their students and may therefore have difficulty accepting the inevitable fact that, given the opportunity, at least some students will cheat. Good will alone, unfortunately, will not impede cheating. Indeed, McKeachie (1994) reported that the most common reasons students give for engaging in academic dishonesty are that they believed other students were cheating and the instructor did not care enough to stop that behavior. Even students who cheat overwhelmingly believe that faculty should care about cheating (Davis et al., 1992). Apparently, the perception that faculty are indifferent to cheating increases students' feelings of inequity. As discussed earlier, equity theory suggests that students who perceive faculty indifference to others' cheating may themselves cheat as a way to reduce the inequity. Hence, taking precautions against cheating is, in itself, an important deterrent. More generally, people cannot perform a behavior if there is no opportunity to do so. For these reasons, instructors should develop strategies that encourage honesty in their courses. Many of the suggestions we provide below apply mainly to institutions without an honor code and some are more applicable for larger classes.

Cheating on exams. To prevent cheating on tests, instructors need to begin at the exam preparation stage. First, exam questions should be changed on a regular basis and students should be made aware of that policy. Campus student organizations may keep files of old exams or course veterans may share with the current class. Second, particularly for large classes, multiple forms of the exam should be prepared. For multiple-choice tests, this is often accomplished by changing the order of the pages or the exam items, but research suggests that the most effective deterrent is to also scramble the order of the alternatives within items (Houston, 1983). Considering alternate forms for essay exams is also worthwhile, although it is more difficult to ensure equality of item difficulty. McKeachie (1994) suggested that when norm-referenced grading is used, establishing separate sets of grade cutoffs for each version of the exam can alleviate this potential problem. Finally, be sure copies of the exam are secure. Eager students may search trash bins, instructor's mailboxes, or even computer disks for previews of the test. Further, if you use a test bank, be certain it is secure. It only takes a moment to remove a copy of that resource from the instructor's office.

Careful test preparation should be followed by careful administration of the test, particularly with large class sections. A well-managed test can significantly reduce the stress that can lead to cheating (McKeachie, 1994). If the room does not allow students to spread out, alternate forms of the exam should be used so that chances for copying are minimized. Often, a checkerboard arrangement, which results in students on all sides having alternate forms, is effective. In other classroom arrangements, however, eyes might easily wander across diagonals. To reduce the time required to distribute the test, instructors and teaching assistants can pre-count exams for each row of seats. The instructor is then better able to ensure that alternate forms are properly distributed and that the appropriate form of the answer sheet accompanies each exam. Also, as students enter the room, test proctors can direct students to ensure that a desired seating plan, such as leaving alternate seats empty, is followed. Finally, students' desktops should contain only the materials needed for the exam. Other books and notes should be stored in backpacks, under seats, or otherwise out of reach.

During the exam, students should be closely monitored, a practice that students view as an effective deterrent to cheating (Davis et al., 1992). Students should see the instructor or proctor walking around the room and watching for inappropriate behavior. For large sections, having more than one proctor is advisable. To reduce the perception that their careful attention indicates distrust, instructors can convey a sense of "alert helpfulness" (McKeachie, 1994), such as by telling students that they can ask proctors for clarification of test questions; this procedure may also encourage reticent students to ask questions. Careful monitoring is also important in smaller classes. Although, as mentioned, smaller classes may have developed norms against cheating, the unpleasant fact remains that students can and do cheat in classes of all sizes.

Finally, students may feel increased control and therefore less motivation to cheat if allowed to use notes during exams. Although this procedure might lead to fears of grade inflation, allowing students to use notes during exams has no effect on average exam scores (Hindman, 1980; Whitley, 1995).

Cheating on Assignments. Assignments completed outside of class provide even greater opportunity to cheat; moreover, what constitutes academic dishonesty may be less clear in these situations. As discussed earlier, the instructor's first charge to is make explicit what constitutes cheating in these situations. As with exam preparation, however, prevention should be the foremost goal. Assignments should be changed or updated regularly and, when necessary, kept secure.

Creative construction of outside assignments is another excellent way to deter academic dishonesty. Whenever possible, assignments should allow room for individualized responses. For example, we both ask students to apply the principles of our discipline to a media event or advertisement. Even if students choose the same news story or ad, interpretation should vary considerably. Similarly, to teach students how to interpret computer printouts of statistical analyses, a colleague has students create their own data so that each outcome is unique.

Another approach is to require documentation of various stages of a project (such as note cards, minutes of group meetings, raw data from a research study) or photocopies of sources (Cole, 1995; Wilhoit, 1994). Finally, although time consuming, instructors may consider requiring multiple drafts of an assignment; this procedure has the additional pedagogical advantage of improving students' writing. As with exams, instructors should assume that students will cheat and, through their actions and words, demonstrate that they care about academic integrity.

Regardless of the grading situation, it is worthwhile to consider authorizing some behaviors that will, in turn, reduce the chances for academic dishonesty. Cooperative learning, for example, has been shown to be an effective learning strategy (Aronson, Blaney, Stephan, Sikes & Snapp, 1978) and adopting this technique can give students a greater sense of control over their work. Finally, students may be reluctant to ask questions about assignments, assuming that they should already have the information and knowledge they need to complete the work. Unfortunately, they may handle any confusion by inappropriately consulting peers or engaging in other forms of academic dishonesty. By communicating to the students that questions are allowed and encouraged, instructors may well discourage cheating. Alternatively, students can be required to cite any help they received in term papers and other assignments (Cole, 1995). Allowing ample class time to solicit relevant questions is one step toward this goal (see Chapter 5). All of these factors may work to increase perceptions of control which, as we noted earlier, may also increase academic integrity.

HANDLING CHEATING

Given the prevalence of academic dishonesty, it seems certain that all instructors will have to deal with this unpleasant situation at one time or another. Those who have considered this possibility ahead of time will find doing so, if not less adversarial, at least more straightforward. The first step should always be familiarizing oneself with the policies and procedures at your institution. Instructors may wish to reprint portions of that policy in their syllabus. In the syllabus, and verbally, instructors should describe how they, personally, are likely to address instances of academic dishonesty. This point cannot be overstated. Without clear written guidelines, faculty may well discover, as one of us did, that an administrator or appeals board will take the student's side on a clear instance of cheating because these procedures were not made explicit. This, in retrospect, does not seem so unreasonable. After all, as we discussed, students are often uninformed as to what constitutes academic dishonesty and faculty have a responsibility to fill that gap.

Unfortunately, policy, in the abstract, rarely addresses the nuances of dealing with instances of real life cheating. Few would doubt that this situation is unpleasant for both instructors and students. Yet if cheating is to be deterred, academic dishonesty must be addressed. In such situations, instructors must first weigh whether cheating clearly occurred or is only suspected. In the latter case, students probably deserve the benefit of the doubt. For example, if a student appears to be looking at another's paper, but the instructor cannot be certain, probably the best way to handle the situation is to simply quietly inform the student that the behavior looks like cheating and that they should stop that behavior. Similarly, if an instructor suspects plagiarism, but cannot be certain, a warning, accompanied by an explanation, is in order.

When evidence is straightforward, however, the best approach is to stick to one's policy and follow through. In our experience, students are well aware that they have cheated and, hence, often choose not to dispute the charge. Some university hearing officers may disagree with this observation, however. Obviously, confronting the student should be as nonadversarial as possible, and students should be given the opportunity to save face. Instructors should be willing to listen to their explanation and not be unduly harsh in their verbal criticism. The best approach is to reiterate the policy and explain in a calm matter the way in which that policy was violated. Instructors should also remind students of their right to due process, outlining the appeals procedure, and directing them to the student ombudsperson or other student advocate. In case the student does question the decision, keep copies of all evidence and any correspondence relevant to the incident. It is good policy to inform relevant administrators about the situation, even if no appeal will be filed.

In many cases, students will remain in the instructor's course or will, perhaps, be students in a future course. Instructors should thus think about how to address future interactions with the assumed guilty parties. Obviously, the best strategy for the future is to forgive and forget. None of us should be forever held accountable for our mistakes. Instructors should let the student know, directly or indirectly, that their relationship with the instructor is not irretrievably damaged. College is a stressful time and faculty should do what they can to alleviate that stress.

IS CHEATING WORTH THE RISK?

As students compare the costs of not cheating (e.g., lower grades than their peers, loss of control over their academic outcomes) to the costs of cheating (e.g., the likelihood of being caught), they may well conclude that the former are higher than the latter. Chances for severe punishment for cheating are indeed low; Maramark and Maline's (1993) review of faculty response to cheating suggested that academic dishonesty is likely handled on an individual basis, with only a minority of cases being referred to the campus judicial system. More telling, perhaps, is data suggesting faculty may overlook cheating altogether. One survey of faculty (Tabachnick, Keith-Spiegel, and Pope, 1991) revealed that 21 percent had ignored clear evidence of cheating. Moreover, faculty may disagree about what constitutes cheating and may respond quite differently to the same behavior (Brilliant & Gribben, 1993). Thus, students who conclude that the benefits of cheating outweigh the risks may not be far off the mark. In addition, the punishment for cheating may be perceived as trivial. Penalties for cheating most often include confronting the student, lowering the student's grade, or issuing a warning (Nuss, 1984, cited in Maramark & Maline, 1993). These may be unpleasant, but are probably not severe enough to reduce cheating. Even if academic dishonesty results in a failing grade, students in many institutions can simply retake the course.

Because it is unlikely that student cheating will have adverse effects, it follows that students are unlikely to know someone who was severely disciplined for cheating. Privacy requirements mean that even those cases that do reach the judicial system cannot be publicly discussed. Obviously advocating publicity for those cases in any manner that violates confidentiality is inappropriate, yet the need to maintain privacy undoubtedly contributes to the perception that there are no real consequences for academic dishonesty. In Chapter 7, McCabe and Pavela discuss in more detail how such institutional policies affect academic integrity.

Since students are unlikely to perceive negative consequences for cheating, using the threat of punishment may have little impact on student behavior. Indeed, threatening students may backfire by inducing psychological reactance (Brehm & Brehm, 1981). As noted earlier, many university students are motivated to maintain control over their academic outcomes. In response to perceived threats to that control, students may decide to cheat simply to prove that they can get away with it. Proactive strategies designed to reduce academic dishonesty, such as those described in this chapter, are likely the most effective deterrents to cheating.

CONCLUSIONS

Research suggests that academic dishonesty in higher education is widespread and that faculty are relatively uninformed about causes of cheating or appropriate responses to cheating. Faculty reluctance to address the problem of academic dishonesty may stem from reasons as varied as lack of sufficient evidence, lack of knowledge about institutional procedures, fear of litigation, and beliefs that reporting cheating may adversely affect a student's future (Maramark & Maline, 1993; Keith-Spiegel, Tabachnick & Washburn, 1994). Yet our analysis suggests that academic dishonesty can be curtailed by understanding why and when students cheat and by taking proactive steps to discourage inappropriate behavior in the classroom.

Toward this end, administrators and faculty members must recognize the need for faculty education on the causes of cheating and the techniques students use to cheat (see Mable in Chapter 2). Whether education is best accomplished by the individual faculty member or at the institutional level will vary by the characteristics of each college and university. It seems clear, however, that the most effective change occurs when standards are established and encouraged at the institutional level (Davis et al. 1992; see also McCabe & Pavela, Chapter 7). Some universities offer training sessions for faculty that focus, at least in part, on academic integrity (see Brilliant & Gribben, 1993, for a model). Others provide handbooks that address ethics more generally and/or academic integrity specifically (Keith-Spiegel, Wittig, Perkins, Balogh & Whitley, 1993). To move away from the punishment model for addressing academic dishonesty, our colleague, Patricia Keith-Spiegel, is developing a "cheaters' school" with the idea that students who cheat should learn about appropriate behavior rather than merely face penalties for such behavior. Although institutional responses to cheating may vary widely, having clearly articulated campus policies and procedures for dealing with academic dishonesty is imperative for successful reduction of the problem.

Regardless of the institutional response, however, each instructor should take responsibility for addressing academic dishonesty in the classroom. To do so, instructors can consider issues raised in this chapter, such as whether course requirements and performance standards are appropriate, whether assignments and exams have been developed to reduce the likelihood of cheating, and whether what constitutes academic dishonesty has been clearly articulated. Furthermore, instructors should consider the impression they make on students. Instructors who come across as demanding or unfair may be inviting academic dishonesty whereas instructors who come across as understanding and fair may discourage cheating. Finally, instructors must take clear preventive steps such as those discussed earlier (e.g., alternate exam forms, changing assignments). Often these steps involve more work for faculty but the payoffs in terms of reduced cheating are worth the effort.

Before the problem of academic dishonesty can be fully addressed, social science research with strong theoretical underpinnings is needed. When causes of cheating have been clearly articulated, more effective ways to reduce the incidence of academic dishonesty can be instituted. These solutions can then be systematically examined to determine which ones best meet the needs of faculty and students with the ultimate goal of establishing a fair and honest educational environment.

References

Aronson, E., Blaney, N., Stephan, C., Sikes, J., and Snapp, M. (1978). *The jigsaw classroom.* Beverly Hills, Calif.: Sage.

Beck, L., and Ajzen, I. (1991). Predicting dishonest actions using the theory of planned behavior. *Journal of Research in Personality, 25,* 285-301.

Brehm, S.S., and Brehm, J.W. (1981). *Psychological reactance: A theory of freedom and control.* New York: Academic Press.

Brilliant, J.J., and Gribben, C.A. (1993). A workshop for faculty and counselors on academic dishonesty. *Journal of College Student Development, 34,* 437-438.

Cole S. (Ed.). (1995). *Four committee papers from the October 1994 conference on academic integrity.* Stanford, Calif.: Center for Academic Integrity, Stanford University.

Davis, S., Grover, C., Becker, A., and McGregor, L. (1992). Academic dishonesty: Prevalence, determinants, techniques, and punishments. *Teaching of Psychology, 19,* 16-20.

Davis, S.F., and Ludvigson, H.W. (1995). Additional data on academic dishonesty and a proposal for remediation. *Teaching of Psychology, 22,* 119-121.

DeMore, S.W., Fisher, J.D., and Baron, R.M. (1988). The equity-control model as a predictor of vandalism among college students. *Journal of Applied Social Psychology, 18,* 80-91.

Eisenberger, R. (1992). Learned industriousness. *Psychological Review, 99,* 248-267.

Fass, R. A. (1990). Cheating and plagiarism. In W. May (Ed.), *Ethics and higher education* (pp. 170-184). New York: Macmillan.

Fiske, S.T., and Taylor, S.E. (1991). *Social cognition* (2nd ed.). New York: McGraw-Hill.

Greenberg, J. (1990). Employee theft as a reaction to underpayment inequity: The hidden cost of pay cuts. *Journal of Applied Psychology, 75,* 561-568.

Greenberg, J. (1993). Stealing in the name of justice: Informational and interpersonal moderators of theft reactions to underpayment inequity. *Organizational Behavior and Human Decision Processes, 54,* 81-103.

Gronlund, N. E. (1993). *How to make achievement tests and assessments* (5th ed.). Boston: Allyn & Bacon.

Haines, V., Diekhoff, G., LaBeff, E., and Clark, R. (1986). College cheating: Immaturity, lack of commitment, and the neutralizing attitude. *Research in Higher Education, 25,* 342-354.

Hindman, C.D. (1980). Crib notes in the classroom: Cheaters never win. *Teaching of Psychology, 7,* 166-168.

Houston, J.P. (1983). Alternate test forms as a means of reducing multiple-choice answer copying in the classroom. *Journal of Educational Psychology, 75,* 572-575.

Keith-Spiegel, P., Tabachnick, B., and Washburn, J. (1994). *Reasons for avoiding confrontation with academic dishonesty.* Unpublished data, Department of Psychological Science, Ball State University.

Keith-Spiegel, P., Wittig, A., Perkins, D., Balogh, D., and Whitley, B., Jr. (1993). *The ethics of teaching: A casebook.* Muncie, Ind.: Ball State University Press.

Lipson, A., and McGavern, N. (1993). *Undergraduate academic dishonesty at MIT: Results of a study of undergraduates, faculty, and graduate teaching assistants.* Cambridge: Massachusetts Institute of Technology. (ERIC Document Reproduction Service No. ED 368 272)

Maramark, S., and Maline, M.B. (1993). *Issues in education: Academic dishonesty among college students.* Washington, D.C.: U.S. Department of Education.

May, K.M., and Loyd, B.H. (1993). Academic dishonesty: The honor system and students' attitudes. *Journal of College Student Development, 34,* 125-129.

McCabe, D.L. (1992). The influence of situational ethics on cheating among college students. *Sociological Inquiry, 62,* 365-374.

McCabe, D.L., and Trevino, L.K. (1993). Academic dishonesty: Honor codes and other contextual influences. *Journal of Higher Education, 64,* 522-538.

McKeachie, W.J. (1994). *Teaching tips: A guidebook for the beginning college teacher* (9th edition). Lexington, Mass.: D.C. Heath.

Mowday, R.T. (1991). Equity theory predictions of behavior in organizations. In R.M. Steers & L.W. Porter (Eds.), *Motivation and work behavior* (5th ed., pp. 111-131). New York: McGraw-Hill.

Roig, M., and Hill, P. (1995, March). *Can college undergraduates determine whether text has been plagiarized?* Paper presented at the annual meeting of the Eastern Psychological Association, Boston.

Tabachnick, B., Keith-Spiegel, P., and Pope, K. (1991). Ethics of teaching: Beliefs and behaviors of psychologists as educators. *American Psychologist, 46,* 506-515.

Whitley, B.E., Jr. (1995). Does "cheating" help? The effect of authorized crib notes during examinations. *College Student Journal, 30,* 489-493.

Wilhoit, S. (1994). Helping students avoid plagiarism. *College Teaching, 42,* 161-164.

5

A COMPREHENSIVE APPROACH FOR CREATING A CAMPUS CLIMATE THAT PROMOTES ACADEMIC INTEGRITY

LYNN RUDOLPH
LINDA TIMM

Who is responsible for creating a climate and culture that support academic integrity? Previous chapters have suggested that characteristics of the institutional environment play a critical role in determining student cheating behaviors. In this chapter, Rudolph and Timm, each of whom has served as an institutional hearing officer, present a comprehensive community-wide approach with specific intervention strategies to create a campus climate that supports academic integrity.

Higher education continues to be the target of critics who question the manner in which colleges and universities have conducted the business of education. Legislatures have most frequently focused their attention on accountability of fiscal management. Accountability in higher education, however, is also focused on student outcomes and asks such questions as Are students really achieving the end goal for which they and their parents have paid large sums of money (Kuh, 1994)? When faculty certify that a student has fulfilled all of the requirements for a degree, how certain can we be that this signifies mastery of curricular requirements? How likely is it that at least some requirements have been fulfilled by a breach of academic integrity?

It is therefore incumbent upon institutions to reexamine a core value of academia, academic integrity, as outcomes are evaluated. As discussed in the popular press, society has experienced a serious rise in white collar crimes of deception, fraud, and dishonesty. It is not unusual to have reports surface in which data were altered in a research project. Economic analyses are reported in ways to support a political position rather than a neutral position. Financial investments may be misrepresented to increase profits. Scientific discoveries have been falsely reported.

As students enter the world of work, it is important that they bring with them a value of honesty and integrity in the work they produce and in the manner in which they conduct their daily business. This value is instilled in them by the manner in which integrity in their academic work is expected by the college or university. According to Payne and Nantz (1994), "childhood and early school experiences and developing levels of moral reasoning influence managerial and professional values. But the college years appear to be a critical period for educators to try alternative means for the moral and ethical education of future business leaders" (p. 90). The benefits of the educational process of promoting and enforcing academic integrity extend far beyond the institution.

STRATEGIES FOR COMMUNICATING THE IMPORTANCE OF ACADEMIC INTEGRITY

If indeed this core value of academic integrity is to be espoused by a college or university, it must become a part of the culture of the institution. The first step in this process, which is communicating the integrity of the academic process to all members of the community, can be accomplished in many ways. First, it must be reflected in the mission statement of the institution. The mission statement reflects a sense of the character of the institution, as well as the overarching goals of the institution. Within such statements, words reflecting the nature of the academic process signal to all that honesty and integrity are hallmarks of academic life.

External publications, such as admissions marketing and recruiting materials, should also reflect the commitment to academic excellence that includes the integrity of one's work. Publications that reach prospective students provide the first opportunity to understand that there will be expectations regarding an individual's participation in the academic process and that excellence is an ongoing focus of the institution.

As a commitment to academic integrity is developed, it will become interwoven into the historical saga of the institution. It becomes a valued and cherished badge that a student carries away from the institution. Honor codes at colleges and universities play a significant role in the identity of the institution. For example, the University of Virginia is recognized for an honor code that has been in existence for over 150 years. Allen and O'Bryan (1992) describe the honor code as having a permanent impact on students' lives: "It can be a guiding beacon over the course of their life—a source of wisdom and inspiration" (p. 371).

The academic reputation of an institution rests with the accomplishments of the faculty and graduates. Students often comment that it makes them angry to see other students cheating because they feel that it lessens the value of their degree. Certainly faculty do not wish to have students leaving their programs to perform in an unethical professional manner. A student teacher who plagiarizes lesson plans, an accounting student who purchases illegal copies of exams, or a computer science student who misuses the computer accounts of a department are not only negative reflections on their institutions, but anathema to their chosen professions. If left unchallenged, students will continue to believe that their behaviors are not unusual or professionally unacceptable.

Internal communication of the value and expectation of academic integrity is most often left to the code of conduct and faculty manuals. Such one-sided methods of communication are not sufficient. For there to be a true inculturation of the value, better methods of communication must be developed and implemented to promote discussion and understanding of the issue of academic integrity. For example, new student orientation programs can engage students and their parents, along with faculty and staff, in initial discussions of ethical dilemmas that students may face regarding academic integrity.

If there is to be any success in minimizing incidents of academic dishonesty in higher education, it is essential that colleges and universities develop an institutional framework for promoting academic integrity among faculty and students. Students are coming to colleges and universities with academic dishonesty behaviors well established. A recent survey conducted by Who's Who Among American High School Students (1994) of 3,177 high-academic achievers reported that 80 percent of the respondents with an A or B average acknowledged that they had personally cheated during their high school attendance. Of the respondents who admitted to cheating, 93 percent indicated they had never been caught. Meyer (1993) stated, "college teachers and their students often share the misconception that the first day of class is the beginning of a new learning experience. On the contrary, students bring their existing knowledge and beliefs about learning with their notebooks and pens to the first class meeting" (p. 104). The reality is that cheating has evolved into an academic coping skill for students. Moore (1991) reported, "Cheating is not a problem on the American college campus, as you perceive it. It is reality" (p. vii).

CORE COMPONENTS IN ESTABLISHING STANDARDS OF ACADEMIC INTEGRITY

Higher education institutions need to provide core components that establish standards of academic integrity and guide the academic community's response to violations of these standards. The core components include: development of an institutional philosophy regarding academic integrity, an educational component for faculty, publications targeted for faculty and students, and an educational component targeted at students. "Institutions of higher education choosing to address academic dishonesty can benefit from a framework that helps them assess their ethos, policies, and programs from a student development perspective" (Kibler, 1993, p. 11).

Developing an Institutional Philosophy
Colleges and universities must establish community norms wherein academic integrity is a priority that is defined, valued, and promoted to community members. The institutional philosophy begins with a clear, well-developed statement fostering strong adherence to standards of academic integrity. It should further articulate the relationship between academic integrity and the degrees students intend to earn. Furthermore, it should define those behaviors considered academically dishonest. The institution's philosophical foundation or mission is further strengthened by the development of and commitment to a consistent procedural component designed to address incidents of academic misconduct.

Procedure statements should provide for the due process rights of the accused and articulate clear procedures for faculty members and others who are referring incidents for adjudication. Once developed, the institution's philosophy and policy statement regarding academic integrity should be shared and widely distributed throughout the campus community (Gehring & Pavela, 1994). Academic integrity philosophy and policy standards promote genuine student scholarship values and in turn help prepare the student for society and the work force.

Departmental Role in Promoting Academic Integrity

Individual colleges and departmental units play an integral role in the promotion of the institution's academic philosophy. At minimum, the department should actively endorse the institutional philosophy and ensure that faculty members have the necessary information, tools, and support to promote academic integrity and address apparent cases of academic dishonesty. In addition, some academic departments, i.e., professional schools and nursing departments, have expanded academic integrity policies. Ludeman's 1986 study of 208 colleges and universities indicated that 84 percent reported having one academic integrity policy for all departments, 13 percent of the respondents reported having polices that varied by department (Ludeman, 1988). It is essential that such "additional" departmental standards are endorsed by and communicated to the office responsible for conduct administration.

Faculty Role in Promoting Academic Integrity

Faculty members play an important role in promoting academic integrity, as they have the greatest amount of direct academic contact with students and they shape the classroom learning environment. Inclusion of academic integrity policies in faculty handbooks underscores the institutional expectations for faculty to actively create a classroom environment that supports the value of academic integrity.

Faculty members have the unique opportunity to infuse the institution or department's academic integrity philosophy and policy into course syllabus documents and the course itself. Faculty responsibilities include: awareness of the institution's policy, consistency in confrontation, and creation of an academic course environment that "eliminates the need, the rationale, and the opportunity to be dishonest" (Gehring & Pavela, 1994, p. 13). As suggested by Jendrek (1992), faculty should be encouraged to include statements on their syllabi addressing academic integrity expectations, and a discussion related to ethical behaviors would be appropriate during early meetings of all courses.

Students' Role in Promoting Academic Integrity
The student's responsibilities may seem obvious to persons reading this chapter; that is, not to commit acts of academic dishonesty. Additionally, Kibler, Nuss, Patterson, and Pavela (1988) defined two additional areas of responsibility: students who violate standards of academic integrity must take responsibility for their actions; and students who observe acts of dishonesty have the responsibility to report the act. How can we encourage students to accept these responsibilities? This is a complex question because the reasons why students cheat are numerous. The reasons cited most frequently include: ignorance of academic dishonesty policies, different value systems, competition for admission to professional and graduate schools, low likelihood of discovery, course content seemingly not relevant to the student's future goals, lack of a relationship with the instructor, and faculty members' failure to secure testing materials and assignments (Baird, 1980; Gehring & Pavela, 1994; Graham, Monday, O'Brien & Steffen, 1994).

For some students it becomes a challenge, a game of student vs. institution. Others feel pressure to succeed knowing that parents have made a great financial investment and sacrifice to support the cost of a college education. The need to have the best transcript possible to secure a competitive place in the job market is also a factor that motivates students to cheat. Self-esteem may play a significant factor in the student's motivation to commit academic dishonesty (Kibler, 1993). Baird (1980) indicated that "the self-attribution of low ability (poor secondary school preparation, lower SAT scores, decreased admissions standards) has increased the fear of failure. Combined with an exogenous concept of college motivation, one predictable result is cheating" (p. 521). If a student perceives that he/she is unable to compete and do as well as others academically, academic misconduct is more likely to occur. Haines, Diekhoff, LaBeff, and Clark (1986) concluded that there were three factors underlying college cheating: immaturity, lack of commitment to academics, and neutralizing attitude.

Students should be informed and reminded of the value the institution places upon academic integrity, be academically prepared, and actively participate in the "development and enforcement of academic dishonesty policies" (Kibler, 1992, p. 82).

Faculty Education

Inherent in any well-orchestrated institutional plan to promote academic integrity is an educational component for faculty. This educational component should be offered to any individual who teaches within the academic community, from undergraduate teaching assistants to graduate teaching staff through full professors (Kibler et al., 1988). If faculty members are expected to confront academic dishonesty and respond to new technology issues mentioned elsewhere in this monograph (see Chapters 9 and 10 for further information), they must be armed with current information related to academic integrity. It is often assumed that teaching faculty are aware of the prevalence of the problem, the institutional policies and procedures, and techniques needed to deter and detect academic dishonesty. In fact, it is more often the case that they have limited or outdated knowledge of the topic. Currently, research provides staggering data that suggest that academic dishonesty is commonplace to students. Kibler (1994) suggested that based on research studies, "students on most, if not all, campuses cheat on their coursework and tests" (p. 93).

Academic dishonesty is becoming habitual for many of our students. Individuals who engage in academically dishonest behavior use a variety of sophisticated techniques. To respond effectively, teaching staff must be informed about the scope of the problem and methods utilized by defrauders.

Faculty education programs should focus on:
- Review of what motivates students to commit academic dishonesty
- Definitions of academic dishonesty
- Risks of ignoring incidents of academic dishonesty
- Cheating techniques
- Deterrence tips, suggestions for test preparation, test administration and guidelines for developing marking techniques for grading
- Detection tips
- Institutional policies, procedures and support systems
- Confrontation guidelines
- Disciplinary referral guidelines
- New technology issues that affect academic integrity
- Legal information
- Current data both from an institutional perspective (number of academic dishonesty cases the institution reports over a period of time) and a national perspective (national survey results).

This educational component could be achieved in a variety of formats, including frequent in-service presentations, annual workshops, or during initial departmental orientations.

Purdue University is one example of an institution that offers a comprehensive College Teaching Workshop which includes a segment on academic integrity. The major benefit of this workshop is that participants are introduced to the individual who is responsible for student conduct administration on campus. As a result, workshop participants gain not only essential information about academic integrity, but they also establish contact with a resource who can assist them to prepare and respond to academic dishonesty violations.

Faculty Publications
Gehring and Pavela (1994) and Kibler (1994) suggested distributing publications written from the faculty perspective to assist them in deterring and addressing academic misconduct issues. An unpublished survey conducted at Old Dominion University (Burnett and Rudolph, 1993) of more than 100 institutions found a wide variety of institutional academic integrity publications for faculty in use at colleges and universities. The publications ranged in comprehensiveness from brief pamphlets outlining definitions, policies, and procedures to extensive booklets detailing policy, procedures, philosophy, detailed judicial procedures, appeal procedures, and flow charts. The documents all have one element in common: they are intended to provide faculty members with essential information to help deter, detect, and deal with academic integrity issues. These publications provide the necessary framework for faculty members to manage academic integrity within the classroom and serve as a catalyst to prompt faculty to respond to incidents that may occur. Kibler et al. (1988) encourage annual distribution of these types of publications.

Student Education Component
In order for students to incorporate academic integrity within their value systems, it is necessary to do more than publish the disciplinary policy in the student handbook. A wealth of opportunities exists on campuses to engage students in an ongoing dialogue about academic integrity. Faculty members should discuss the topic in every course and within as many contexts as possible. Such discussions should not be restricted to the first day of the course, which unfortunately is often the only time the topic is raised,

if at all, for many students. The discussion can occur frequently throughout the course. Wilhoit (1994) suggested that institutions might be more effective in responding to the problem of academic dishonesty if "more time was spent helping students learn how to avoid it" (p. 161). For example, if a research paper is assigned, it would be appropriate to review guidelines for documentation, quotation, and perhaps some examples of paraphrasing. This is especially important because style guidelines differ depending upon the area of academic study. In addition, faculty members should discuss guidelines for collaboration on assignments. Frequently students argue (at their disciplinary hearing) that professors have differing views of what constitutes collaboration; therefore, it is essential to provide the student with clear expectations.

Nuss (1984) suggested "incorporating a discussion of academic integrity into orientation and student advising sessions" (p. 143). A discussion about academic integrity would parallel the policy and procedure topics that are typically highlighted at orientation programs. Kibler et al. (1988) further supported the concept and suggested that academic integrity discussions be included in all types of orientation programs, including new student, transfer, and international student orientations.

Many institutions have developed publications designed to educate students about academic integrity. These publications typically include:
- The institutional academic integrity statement
- Definitions of academic dishonesty
- Tips to avoid claims of academic dishonesty
- Consequences/sanctions
- Suggestions for reporting incidents of peer academic dishonesty.

Student academic integrity publications should be distributed throughout the campus and certainly could be included in admissions packets and orientation packets. A variety of methods can be utilized to educate students about the risks involved in committing academic dishonesty. Kibler et al. (1988) suggested including academic integrity policies in class schedule booklets, and on examination booklets. Campus newspapers can also serve a vital role in academic dishonesty deterrence through frequent well timed campus newspaper advertisements that warn students of risks and promote academic integrity (Kibler et al, 1988).

While the suggestions previously mentioned focus on items provided by the institution for students, it is important not to underestimate the vital role students can play in educating their peers with regard to academic integrity education. For example, Old Dominion University recently revised its honor code in order to provide faculty with more responsibility for detecting cases of academic dishonesty. To ensure that students maintain a sense of responsibility for supporting the honor system, a peer education component was developed which empowers members of the Honor Board with the responsibility to provide academic integrity education for their peers. As a result, students at Old Dominion are vested in both the educational and adjudication functions of the institution's academic integrity procedures, and faculty are clearly assigned the responsibility for managing integrity within the classroom.

To effectively communicate academic integrity standards to the entire community, key nonacademic staff on campus should be identified and educated to recognize the prevalent nature of student dishonesty, the university's academic integrity policy, and techniques that have proven to be effective in reducing cheating opportunities. The list could include, but is not limited to: deans and department chairs, writing center and math lab staff, undergraduate teaching assistants, and such student leaders as residence hall and peer counselors. Individuals who serve in these roles can infuse a sense of the importance of academic integrity into their interactions with students and may be in a position to detect and or confront violations.

LEARNING ENVIRONMENT

At this point, the focus will turn to methods that faculty members should consider when establishing their educational course environment. These methods should enhance the faculty member's ability to "deter, detect and deal with academic integrity" issues (Akers, 1994, p. 2).

The classroom environment is decisive in its effect on a student's decision to commit an act of academic dishonesty. As Steininger, Johnson, and Kirts (1964) reported, "the more negative a situation, the more subjects considered cheating justified, the more urge they said they would have to cheat, and the more they said they would cheat" (p. 322). A faculty member's individual teaching style and personality can influence the class environment and may have an impact on a student's decision to commit academic dishonesty (Bushway & Nash, 1977; Geist, 1993; Monitor, 1971; Singhal & Johnson, 1983). The following classroom strategies are designed to create a classroom environment that encourages student academic integrity and discourages cheating (Bushway & Nash, 1977; Gehring &

Pavela, 1994; Geist, 1993; Kibler et al., 1988; Monitor, 1971; Singhal & Johnson, 1983):

- Establishing clear course guidelines with relevant course objectives and assignments. If students view courses as fraught with busy work, with assignments bearing no relevance to the overall course, they are inclined to engage in cheating behavior. Monitor (1971) reported that students identified several factors that they feel justify cheating on such exercises as homework: purposelessness, unbalanced workload in courseloads, nongraded assignment; and viewing the work as practice. Faculty members should explain the relevance of assignments to the course goals and to predicted success in the course.

- Eliminating the "all or nothing" (Gehring & Pavela, 1994, p. 13) pressure to succeed at all costs. Frequent testing and or assignments helps to reduce this problem if a student's grade is based on numerous academic exercises, rather than performance on one or two tests.

- Knowing student's ability levels and design course and timing of exams based on knowledge, students are more apt to focus on learning the course material and less on passing the course. Baseline ability can be assessed via writing assignments and quizzes.

- Teaching personality and approachability in the classroom. If a faculty member makes negative statements about students' abilities, discourages student input, demeans students, or is very "authoritarian," students may be more inclined to cheat (Bushway & Nash 1977, p. 628). DeLucia's (1994) survey data of faculty-student relationships indicated that students expressed concern about "being embarrassed, picked on, or unnecessarily provoked in class" (p. 277). Approachability demonstrates that the faculty member is interested in the student and the student's learning. Faculty members can demonstrate this by providing office hours, pretest review sessions, one-on-one exam reviews, and a general willingness to listen to students' views and ideas.

- Recognizing close student-faculty relationships as the single strongest deterrent to cheating, as suggested by Kaplan and Mable in Chapter 2 and Clifford in Chapter 8.

PROCTORING/DETECTION

Appropriate detection methods combined with consistent institutional adjudication procedures should aid faculty members in responding more effectively to disruptive incidents. According to Hardy (1982), "there are countless professors who refuse to address the problem of academic dishonesty. The biggest problem is that professors simply deny that such problems exist" (p. 70). Monitor (1971) implied that faculty may inadvertently "condone cheating by not acting in meaningful ways against it" (p. 97). Many faculty, overloaded with large student sections, research requirements, and the other countless demands of academic life, simply do not want to become involved in an adversarial process with the possibility of lengthy appeals and a decision counter to the faculty view of what actually occurred.

The guidelines that follow expand on the suggestions cited by Whitley and Kite in Chapter 4 and are intended to reduce the likelihood that academic dishonesty will occur in the classroom. The guidelines are based on the authors' experiences as hearing officers and are supported by the literature as noted.

- When administering short-answer or multiple-choice exams, make alternate forms of the exam. If alternate forms are not possible, duplicate the exam on several different colored stocks to give the appearance of alternate exams (Hardy, 1982; Kibler et al., 1988).
- Provide accountability for exam duplication, collation, distribution, and return. Numbering the exams provides an effective method to ensure that all exams are accounted for before, during, and after the examination period (Hardy, 1982; Kibler et al., 1988).
- Maintain a seating chart (if class size allows) that can be used to verify student seating after the exam (Hardy, 1982).
- Be aware of student apparel and accessories during exams. Require individuals wearing baseball caps to remove them or turn the cap around so the bill is not in view, remove sunglasses and portable tape players. If calculators are permitted, attention should be given to programmable calculators (Akers, 1994).
- Faculty members should review blue books by requiring students to submit blank books (signed or unsigned) the day before the exam (Gehring & Pavela 1994; Geist, 1993; Kibler et al., 1988).
- In essay courses, require the student to submit drafts of essays/papers and/or require a documentation review (Geist, 1993; Wilhoit, 1994).

- In some courses, faculty members can minimize the use of unauthorized crib sheets by allowing students to use solution sheets or preapproved notes.
- Clearly mark the exam document as an "exam" on each page and if possible provide a watermark on the exam which makes unauthorized duplication apparent.
- Require student identification prior to exam entry or upon submission of completed exam and/or require student signatures on exams (Gehring & Pavela, 1994; Geist, 1993; Kibler et al., 1988).
- Count the number of students present during the exam and verify with the number of students listed on the official course roster (Kibler et al., 1988).
- Gather numbered exams by row so that exam number and seating location can be verified. Be sure to be consistent in exam collection instructions, e.g., *pass exams to the left and place your exam on top*. A second collection strategy involves requiring students to leave their signed exams, answer sheets, and scrap paper on their desks for collection and verification by proctors (Gehring & Pavela 1994; Geist, 1993).
- Faculty members and all graders should develop a marking system to use during grading. This is especially important if multiple graders are used, to indicate blank answers on exams, and to indicate completion of students' work. Faculty members who use this technique will minimize the occurrences of answer changes and additions after the exam is returned to the student.
- Maintain security of the grade book throughout the course.

CONFRONTATION

Colleges and universities differ in their guidelines and procedures for confronting academic dishonesty during an exam. In addition, some confrontation differences are warranted depending on the type of academic dishonesty that is occurring, i.e. a "ringer" (student A identifies self as student B) in an exam vs. the perception that a student is copying. Some institutions suggest immediate confrontation while others suggest dealing with the incident at the conclusion of an exam. If confrontations are done during the exam, it is essential to minimize the disruption that may occur as a result. Regardless of the institution's confrontation procedures, it is essential for faculty members to gather all relevant information, evidence, and documentation, including observations from other proctors, prior to confronting the student. Faculty members should consult with appropriate campus resource personnel (i.e., dean of students, honor committee representative, or hearing officer) to verify recommended confrontation procedures. In addition, faculty members are encouraged to consult with the resource person after suspected incidents of academic misconduct have occurred to evaluate the incident and determine how best to proceed.

Faculty members' perceptions about academic integrity and their willingness to confront an incident differ and may have an impact on confrontation. An excerpt from a *Synthesis* interview with McCabe (1993) helps illustrate this point. McCabe reported that when faculty were asked how much effort would they go through to document a case of cheating in their course, 60 percent of the faculty at non-honor code schools and 47 percent at schools with honor codes said they would go to little or very little effort to document an incident (p. 343). In addition, the decision to confront may be affected by the faculty member's opinion as to the severity of the incident (Nuss, 1984).

MECHANICS

According to Gehring and Pavela (1994), academic dishonesty falls within four categories: cheating, fabrication, facilitating academic dishonesty, and plagiarism. Within these broad categories exists a varied assortment of behaviors that include:
- Using "ringers" to appear for one exam or for an entire course.
- Using unauthorized information/tools during an exam or academic exercise. Unauthorized notes have been found dictated on a portable tape recorder; written on the back of mirrored sunglasses, false fingernails, calculator covers, body parts, baseball cap bills, classroom desks and chairs (prior to the exam); and programmed into calculators.
- Using verbal or nonverbal signals during an exam.
- Copying from another student during an exam or academic exercise.
- Stealing completed assignments and submitting them as one's own work.

- Stealing the professors grade book and altering grades.
- Stealing exams and/or course exam manuals.
- Altering scored tests during test reviews.
- Collaborating without permission, especially on computer assignments.

Obviously the list is not inclusive of all the possible types of academic dishonesty. It provides, however, a sample of the varying degrees of academic dishonesty that are occurring on college and university campuses.

POLICY AND PROCEDURES ISSUES

Academic integrity requires a strong and united institutional commitment if it is to survive in the face of the many pressures that lead students to cheat. A strong philosophy regarding the adjudication of academic dishonesty must be accepted and supported at all levels of the institution, especially among faculty. Communicating this commitment can be accomplished in many ways. Brochures, statements on a course syllabus, a student code of conduct, information on electronic mail or web sites, and course registration booklets are media that have been used effectively on some campuses.

Other less used but very effective ways of conveying an institution's priority for academic integrity are disciplinary policy review sessions with faculty and students, focus groups of faculty and students, and surveys of faculty and students about the confrontation and adjudication of academic dishonesty. Written follow-up with individual faculty members after a case has been completed is helpful in bringing closure to the case.

One additional method of involving faculty and students in the process is to institute a post-adjudication evaluation. Participants' perceptions and feelings in the adjudication process can provide valuable data for assessing and understanding the reluctance to refer cases for adjudication and for recognizing modifications that may provide for a more educationally sound process.

Geist (1993) indicated that it is important to build a sense of trust with faculty as they confront cases of academic dishonesty. She provided several suggestions for building that relationship, including the value of personal follow-up with faculty members after the adjudication of a case of academic dishonesty. Many times a faculty member may need to reassess how tests are administered, how assignments are given, or how to better develop a classroom environment that fosters academic integrity. Judicial officers and/or honor committee representatives should be campus-based consultants for faculty as they struggle for answers to these concerns.

Heightening the awareness that academic dishonesty will not be tolerated and will result in a disciplinary challenge is a valuable deterrent and an educationally sound principle. Using the campus newspaper to communicate aggregate data on cases of academic dishonesty and subsequent disciplinary actions provides the academic community with the feedback that such violations are taken seriously, are adjudicated, and that consequences will result from such behaviors.

STUDENT CONSIDERATIONS

Students provide valuable information that can be useful in the understanding of cheating behavior. Numerous studies have been conducted in which students are asked to self-report information regarding frequency of cheating, types of cheating behaviors, and attitudes regarding cheating. This data is essential as a basis for developing ways to educationally address the ethical and moral dilemmas the students express in their responses (See Chapter 1 for further information).

Simply improving test administration and assignment validity only creates barriers to cheating. If lasting results are to be realized, there must be ongoing discussions of ethics and values in order to challenge students to examine their personal views and behaviors. One institution that has such a program is the United States Naval Academy. As a result of a much publicized cheating scandal, a mandatory character development program has been instituted. Ideally, programs of this nature should be instituted as a proactive measure rather than a reactive solution to incidents of academic misconduct. Initiating dialogue between students and faculty is the key to success. Jendrek (1992) supported this claim and stated that "the encouragement of open discussion among faculty members and students about academic dishonesty and its consequences will do more to enable higher education to achieve its goals than by simply setting up roadblocks to cheating. Open discussions may encourage students (and faculty) to move from indifference to a personal commitment to ethical principals" (p. 272).

CONCLUSIONS

Academic integrity is shared responsibility for all members of our educational communities (Gehring & Pavela, 1994; Kibler et al., 1988; Nuss, 1994). Gehring and Pavela (1994) further stated that "it is an ongoing and continual effort — not a one-shot response" (p. 12). It is hoped that this chapter provided a template for community members to refer to when developing and reviewing strategies designed to promote and respond to academic integrity issues. We must actively create opportunities for faculty, students, and staff to discuss, be involved in, and be educated about academic integrity if we are to successfully address the problem on our campuses.

References

Akers, S. (1994). Deterring, detecting, and dealing with academic dishonesty. [Brochure]. West Lafayette, Ind.

Allen, W., and O'Bryan, S. (1992). Building a community of trust: The single sanction at Virginia. *Synthesis: Law and Policy in Higher Education, 356,* 370-371.

Baird, J.S. (1980). Current trends in college cheating. *Psychology in the Schools, 17,* 515-522.

Burnett, D., and Rudolph, L. (1993). "Academic Misconduct Survey." Unpublished raw data.

Bushway, A., and Nash, W.R. (1977). School cheating behavior. *Review of Educational Research, 47,* 623-632.

DeLucia, R.C. (1994). Perceptions of faculty-student relationships: A survey. *NASPA Journal, 31,* 271-279.

Gehring, D., and Pavela, G. (1994). *Issues and Perspectives on Academic Integrity.* (2nd ed.). Washington, DC: National Association of Student Personnel Administrators.

Geist, N.K. (1993). Confronting cases of academic dishonesty — Where policy and practice meet. *Synthesis: Law and Policy in Higher Education,* 348-349.

Graham, M.A., Monday, J. O'Brien, K., and Steffen, S. (1994). Cheating at small colleges: An examination of student and faculty attitudes and behaviors. *Journal of College Student Development, 35,* 255-260.

Haines, V., Deikhoff, G., LaBeff, E., and Clark, R. (1986). College cheating: Immaturity, lack of commitment, and the neutralizing attitude. *Research in Higher Education, 25*(4), 342-354.

Hardy, R.J. (1982). Preventing academic dishonesty: Some important tips for political science professors. *Teaching Political Science, 9,* 68-77.

Jendrek, M.P. (1992). Students' reactions to academic dishonesty. *Journal of College Student Development, 33,* 260-273.

Kibler, W., Nuss, E., Paterson, B., and Pavela, G. (1988). *Academic integrity and student development: Legal issues, policy perspectives.* Asheville, N.C.: College Administration Publications.

Kibler, W.L. (1992, November 11). Cheating: Institutions need a comprehensive plan for promoting academic integrity. *The Chronicle of Higher Education,* pp. B1-B2.

Kibler, W.L. (1993). A framework for addressing academic dishonesty from a student development perspective. *NASPA Journal, 31,* 8-18.

Kibler, W.L. (1994). Addressing academic dishonesty: What are institutions of higher education doing and not doing. *NASPA Journal, 31,* 92-101.

Kuh, G. (1994). "The Student Learning Imperative: Implications for Student Affairs." [ACPA-sponsored project].

Ludeman, R.B. (1988). A survey of academic integrity practices in U.S. higher education. *Journal of College Student Development, 29,* 172-173.

McCabe, D.L. (1993). Academic integrity: What the latest research shows. *Synthesis: Law and Policy in Higher Education,* 340-343.

Meyer, D.K. (1993). Recognizing and changing students' misconceptions: An instructional perspective. *College Teaching, 41,* 104-108.

Moore, M. (1991). *Cheating 101: The benefits and fundamentals of earning the easy "A."* Hopewell, N.J.: Moore & Moore Publishing.

Monitor, K. (1971). Cheating in high school. *School and Society, 99,* 96-98.

Nuss, E.M. (1984). Academic integrity: Comparing faculty and student attitudes. *Improving College & University Teaching, 32*(3), 140-144.

Payne, S.L., and Nantz, K.S. (1994). Social accounts and metaphors about cheating. *College Teaching, 42,* 90-96.

Singhal, A.C., and Johnson, P. (1983). How to halt student dishonesty. *College Student Journal, 17,* 13-19.

Steininger, M., Johnson, R., and Kirts, D. (1964). Cheating on college examinations as a function of situationally aroused anxiety and hostility. *Journal of Educational Psychology, 55,* 317-324.

Who's Who Among American High School Students: Twenty-fifth Survey of High Achievers. (1994). Lake Forest, IL., Educational Communications, Inc.

Wilhoit, S. (1994). Helping students avoid plagiarism. *College Teaching, 42,* 161-164.

6

WHEN INSTITUTIONS AND THEIR FACULTY ADDRESS ISSUES OF ACADEMIC DISHONESTY

Realities and Myths

Donald D. Gehring

Up to this point, we have focused on several issues that define how and why we should address academic integrity. One compelling area that merits further review and commentary is the legal issues that impact the entire educational community. Gehring highlights legal topics that provide important guidelines for anyone dealing with academic integrity violations and are particularly relevant for faculty members.

Protecting the integrity of the academic processes should be a primary concern of every institution of higher education and every faculty member; however, studies have shown that student cheating continues to be a major problem on campus (Collison, 1990a; Collison, 1990b; Jendrek, 1989; McCabe, 1993; McCabe & Trevino, 1993). Some commentators refer to the situation as "serious" (Gehring & Pavela, 1995), while others consider cheating on campus to be of "epidemic" proportions (Wellborn, 1980).

Chapters in this monograph describe a prevalence of cheating ranging from citation oversight to using "ringers" to take exams. College presidents at every type of institution, on the other hand, consider "violations of honor codes or rules of academic integrity" to be in the main even less than a moderate problem (Boyer, 1990). This chapter focuses on the realities of faculty addressing issues of academic dishonesty on public and private campuses. It includes the legal basis for confronting the issue and the process that is due accused students. The chapter also delineates the real risk of liability to faculty who choose to confront instances of academic dishonesty on their own without following campus procedures. Finally, several myths associated with reporting academic dishonesty are debunked.

LEGAL BASIS FOR PROTECTING ACADEMIC INTEGRITY

Although there seems to be a disagreement among researchers, commentators, and practitioners about the extent of cheating on campus, this disparity does not reduce the responsibility of institutions for maintaining the integrity of academic processes. The legal basis for carrying out this responsibility has consistently been recognized by the judiciary. The U.S. District Court for the western district of Missouri in setting forth a *General Order on Judicial Standards of Procedure and Substance in Review of Student Discipline in Tax Supported Institutions of Higher Education* (1968) listed among the "Lawful Missions of Tax Supported Institutions of Higher Education" the teaching of ethical values. Furthermore, the court stated:

> No student may, without liability to lawful discipline, intentionally act to impair or prevent the accomplishment of any lawful mission, process, or function of an educational institution (p. 141).

Finally, the court noted that institutions may establish standards relevant to their lawful missions which may "require superior ethical and moral behavior" (p. 145). Other courts have viewed disciplining students for cheating as an institution's inherent right (*Slaughter v. Brigham Young University*, 1975; *Esteban v. Central Missouri State College*, 1968; *State v. Hyman*, 1942). Colleges and universities, therefore, not only have a responsibility to uphold the integrity of academic processes, but they have a legally recognized basis for doing so. This legal basis to discipline for violations of standards of academic integrity, however, is not unfettered but, at least for public institutions, must conform to the Constitutional requirements of the Fourteenth Amendment's due process clause.

DUE PROCESS AND ACADEMIC INTEGRITY AT PUBLIC INSTITUTIONS

The Fourteenth Amendment, in part, "prohibits states or their agents (public colleges and universities) from depriving . . . any person of life, liberty or property without due process of law." The landmark case of *Dixon v. Alabama State Board of Education* (1961) held that before students at a public college or university could be subjected to long-term suspension or expulsion they were entitled to Fourteenth Amendment due process protections. Even well before *Dixon,* the judiciary recognized continuing enrollment at a public institution as a "property interest" that could not be deprived without due process. In *State v. Hyman* (1942) the Supreme Court of Tennessee conceded, in a case involving students who were expelled for selling final exam questions to their classmates, that ". . . the right to study medicine and practice medicine is a property right . . ." (p. 827). Furthermore, students have a liberty interest in their good name, reputation, honor or integrity, and the U.S. Supreme Court has said that minimum due process must be provided "where a person's good name, reputation, honor or integrity is at stake because of what the government is doing to him" (*Wisconsin v. Constantineau,* 1971, p. 437).

> Due process, however, is not a fixed concept, but rather defined "by the gradual process of judicial inclusion and exclusion" (*Davidson v. New Orleans,* 1877, p. 104). The process that is due depends upon the nature of the right that may be deprived (*University of Texas Med. School v. Than,* 1994). Thus, students who may be suspended or expelled should be afforded a good deal of process. The Fifth Circuit Court of Appeals set forth the general parameters for due process in instances where students could be suspended for a long period of time or expelled.
>
> For the guidance of the parties in the event of further proceedings, we state our views on the nature of the notice and hearing required by due process prior to expulsion from a state college or university. They should, we think, comply with the following standards. The notice should contain a statement of the specific charges and grounds which, if proven, would justify expulsion under the regulations of the Board of Education. The nature of the hearing should vary depending upon the circumstances of the particular case. The case before us requires something more than an informal interview with an administrative authority of the college. By its nature, a charge of misconduct, as opposed to a failure to meet the scholastic standards of the college, depends upon a collection of the facts concerning the charged misconduct, easily colored by the point of view of the witnesses. In such circumstances, a hearing which gives the Board or the administrative authorities of

the college an opportunity to hear both sides in considerable detail is best suited to protect the rights of all involved. This is not to imply that a full-dress judicial hearing, with the right to cross-examine witness is required. Such a hearing, with the attending publicity and disturbance of college activities, might be detrimental to the college's educational atmosphere and impractical to carry out. Nevertheless, the rudiments of an adversary proceeding may be preserved without encroaching upon the interests of the college. In the instant case, the student should be given the names of the witnesses against him and an oral or written report on the facts to which each witness testifies. He should also be given the opportunity to present to the Board, or at least to an administrative official of the college, his own defense against the charges and to produce either oral testimony or written affidavits of witnesses in his behalf. If the hearing is not before the Board directly, the results and findings of the hearing should be presented in a report open to the student's inspection. If these rudimentary elements of fair play are followed in a case of misconduct of this particular type, we feel that the requirements of due process of law will have been fulfilled (*Dixon v. Alabama State Board of Education,* 1961, p. 158).

The standards outlined in *Dixon* for ". . . minimum due process requirements for disciplinary hearings in an academic setting [are] still accurate today" (*Henson v. Honor Committee of U. Va.*, 1983, p. 74).

The distinction made by the court between ". . . a charge of misconduct as opposed to a failure to meet the scholastic standards . . ." (*Dixon v. Alabama State Board of Education,* 1961, p. 158) has been viewed by some as a signal that issues of academic integrity involve scholastic standards and are thereby not subject to the strictures of due process. This reasoning is a mistake. As Pavela (1988) pointed out, the U.S. Supreme Court has drawn a distinction between disciplinary and academic decision making:

- an academic evaluation "is by its nature more subjective and evaluative" than the "typical factual questions" encountered in the "average disciplinary decision"
- disciplinary proceedings "automatically" bring "an adversarial flavor to the normal student-teacher relationship. The same conclusion does not follow in the academic context" (p. 38).

The difference between an academic evaluation and a determination of misconduct was clearly outlined by the Texas Court of Appeals in a case involving a medical student accused of cheating by copying from another student's exam. The court observed that while cheating always arises in an academic context that only ". . . speaks to the backdrop of the act of cheating, not to the nature of the act itself. . . . Cheating is a misdeed" (*University of Texas Med. School v. Than*, 1994, p. 844). The court elaborated on the distinction by noting:

> A potential consequence of a misdeed is punishment. However, it is not a misdeed to perform unsatisfactorily at one's studies or activities related to those studies. . . . Academic dismissal occurs when the student did not achieve the minimum standards by which the student's fitness to practice the profession for which he or she is preparing are measured [citations omitted]. In such a case, dismissal is not punishment; it is discarding as unfit. Dismissal for a misdeed, however, is punitive. It is therefore disciplinary, not academic. A dismissal for the misdeed of cheating is a disciplinary dismissal (p. 844).

Regardless of whether violations of academic integrity standards are characterized as academic discipline or simply discipline, students accused of cheating must be afforded due process (*Jones v. Board of Governors of University of N.C.*, 1983; *State v. Hyman*, 1942; *Roberts v. Knowlton*, 1974; *Kalinsky v. State University of New York*, 1990; *James v. Wall*, 1989; *McDonald v. Board of Trustees of University of Illinois*, 1974; *Lightsey v. King*, 1983). While the *Dixon* court set out the general parameters for procedural due process, there have been many refinements to those general standards since 1961.

THE PROCESS THAT IS DUE

Notice of the Alleged Violation

The notice of changes should be in writing since an oral notification could be misunderstood and "A written notice of the precise charges will remedy this situation" (*Esteban v. Central Missouri State College*, 1967, p. 651). The notice should be sent to the last official address provided by the student *(Wright v. Texas Southern University*, 1968). Institutions should have administrative regulations requiring students to maintain a current address in the registrar's office. The violation cited in the notice should be specific enough to permit the student to prepare a defense against it (*Scott v. Alabama State Board of Education*, 1969). Simply charging a student with "cheating" may run afoul of due process if challenged and it would be preferable to say specifically what form of cheating was involved, e.g., copying from the exam of Mr. Doe or using a crib sheet during the exam.

On the other hand, the Military Academy code which provides that "A cadet will not lie, cheat or steal or tolerate those who do" has been upheld as being a clear statement of what is prohibited (*White v. Knowlton*, 1973, p. 449). Even "conduct incompatible with . . . principles of academic integrity" listed in the Student Code has been upheld where were students talking with each other during an exam (*Boehm v. U. of Pa. School of Vet. Med.*, 1990, p. 584).

A list of definitions of various types of academic dishonesty should also be incorporated in the student handbook or other official documents (see Gehring & Pavela, 1994, for examples). Finally, the notice should be sent to the student as soon as possible. Long delays in notifying students that they are being formally charged with violating the institution's academic integrity policy could put the student at a disadvantage in preparing a defense and therefore held to be a violation of due process. In a case involving a medical student, who was not informed until 18 days after the exam that he was "accused of cheating" and not formally notified how he had allegedly cheated until 41 days after the exam, the court held that his due process rights were violated because the school did not give him timely notice (*University of Texas Med. School v. Than,* 1994).

Hearing

There should be enough time between the notice and the hearing to allow the student to prepare a defense. The hearing should provide students with an opportunity to defend themselves, and the hearing must be before an unbiased person or persons (*Harvey v. Palmer College of Chiropractic,* 1984).

Right to Counsel

There is no absolute right to counsel in cases of academic dishonesty (*Henson v. Honor Committee of U. Va.*, 1983). Where a medical student complained that his due process rights were violated when he was not permitted legal counsel to represent him, the court responded by noting:

> ... the interests of a tax supported state institution in an orderly procedure confined to its own community for the handling of instances of alleged academic dishonesty is not to be regarded lightly. Judicial reluctance to force the inclusion of a non-university individual into the delicate decision making process should be that much greater where, as here, the procedures involve elaborate efforts to insure that a fair result is reached. The Court is of the view that a determination as to the academic honesty of a student is analogous to the determination of professional competency of a professor and is a matter peculiarly within the discretion of a college administration (*Garshnau v. The Pennsylvania State University,* 1975, p. 921).

Although there is no absolute right to representation by legal counsel, unusual circumstances may require it. For example, if the institution uses legal counsel to present its case the student should also be allowed to have legal representation to maintain the essence of due process — fundamental fairness. Also, institutions that allow students to have advisors but do not specify that those advisors may not be legal counsel should not prohibit them from attending the hearing. However, where counsel is serving in an advisor's role they should be informed at the beginning of the hearing of the limits of their participation. It is generally recommended that academic dishonesty hearings not permit legal counsel for either side or even as advisors.

Standard of Proof
It has been argued that the standard of "substantial evidence" should be applied in student discipline cases (*Jackson v. Hayakawa,* 1985) and even in academic dishonesty cases (*Kalinsky v. State University of New York,* 1990). However, one court argued very forcefully that while the "substantial evidence" standard should be used in disciplinary situations involving conduct "falling within the scope of any constitutional protection," the offense of academic dishonesty is "unique to the academic community" and federal courts should uphold decisions based on "some evidence" (*McDonald v. Board of Trustees of the University of Illinois,* 1974, p. 104). Again, in keeping with the spirit of due process as fundamental fairness the "preponderance of the evidence" would be a good standard to apply. A preponderance of evidence is anything more than half. Clearly the "beyond a reasonable doubt" standard should never be used in student disciplinary hearings either academic or other since it is only applicable in criminal proceedings and "the attempted analogy of student discipline to criminal proceedings against adults and juveniles is not sound" (*General Order,* 1968, p. 142).

Sanctions
The courts generally will not interfere with the judgment of institutional officials unless it can be shown that there has been a clear abuse of discretion, arbitrary or capricious treatment (*Slaughter v. Brigham Young University,* 1975). This is equally true for sanctions imposed for academic dishonesty. Even where the only punishment for cheating was expulsion, the courts have upheld the sanction and said that it did not constitute cruel and unusual punishment (*Roberts v. Knowlton,* 1974). In a plagiarism case at Princeton University involving an otherwise outstanding student whose

punishment was to defer her graduation for a year, the court said:

> Plaintiff claims that the penalty is supposed to provide something educative in its imposition. She argues that the penalty here is improper because there is no educational value to be found in it. Perhaps plaintiff's self-concern blinds her to the fact that the penalty imposed on her, as a leader of the University community, has to have some educative effect on other student members of the community. In addition to paraphrase the poet, "the child is mother to the woman," we believe that the lesson to be learned here should be learned by Gabrielle Napolitano and borne by her for the rest of her life. We are sure it will strengthen her in her resolve to become a success in whatever endeavor she chooses (*Napolitano v. Trustees of Princeton University*, 1982, p. 278-279).

In addition, not all sanctions need to be the same. "Each penalty obviously must be tailored to the offense committed, and the offense committed must be viewed with regard to the offender and the community" (*Napolitano v. Trustees of Princeton University,* 1982, p. 278). However, once a student is found not to have committed an act of academic dishonesty faculty must abide by that decision regardless of their personal opinions. Taking any sort of action against a student found to be innocent of academic dishonesty would constitute a violation of due process, for "there is no difference between failing to provide a due process hearing and providing one but ignoring the outcome" (*Lightsey v. King*, 1983, p. 649).

Transcriptions
Whether to keep a transcript is another issue in considering the process that is due. Although there is no right to appeal a decision in campus judicial proceedings, it would be good practice to have someone review suspensions or expulsions. This is not to say that there must be elaborate appellate bodies or multiple levels of appeal. If the decision to suspend or expel is to be reviewed, however, some type of transcript of the hearing should be provided to the person or persons reviewing the decision. The courts have held that there is no requirement to keep a tape recording or other transcription of the hearing (*Mary M. v. Clark,* 1984; *Sohmer v. Kinnard,* 1982), but good practice suggests making a verbatim recording of the hearing (Stoner & Cerminara, 1990).

RESPONDING TO ACADEMIC DISHONESTY AT PRIVATE INSTITUTIONS

The procedural protections discussed above derive from the Fourteenth Amendment's due process clause, but the U.S. Supreme Court said the Constitution "erects no shield against purely private conduct" (*Shelly v. Kraemer*, 1947, p. 1180). The rights found in the Bill of Rights and other amendments do not apply to private institutions unless they are found to be engaged in "state action." There have been many attempts to show "state action" on the part of private institutions, but to no avail (Gehring, 1993).

Contractual Relationship
The relationship between private colleges and universities and their students is essentially one of contract (*Corso v. Creighton University*, 1984). This contractual relationship is both implied and express. "The essence of the implied contract is that an academic institution must act in good faith in its dealings with students" (*Olsson v. Board of Higher Education*, 1980, p. 251). Acting in good faith would seem to imply that private institutions have fair procedures for adjudicating offenses of academic dishonesty. Several courts have said that students accused of cheating should be treated in a fundamentally fair manner (*Clayton v. Trustees of Princeton University*, 1985; *Boehm v. U. of Pa. School of Vet. Med.*, 1990). The express contract is written and the terms and conditions should be found in the official publications (*Babcock v. New Orleans Baptist Theological Seminary*, 1989; *Lexington Theological Seminary v. Vance*, 1979; *Steinberg v. Chicago Medical School*, 1977; *Corso v. Creighton University*, 1984). Thus, private institutions must adhere to the procedures outlined in their handbooks or other official publications or risk breach of contract. Creighton University stated in its handbook that where a serious penalty may result students were entitled to a hearing before the discipline committee and an appeal to the president. Salvatore Corso, a medical student, was accused of cheating on an exam and suspended by the acting dean without a hearing. The Eighth Circuit Court of Appeals held that Creighton had breached its contract with Corso and ordered it to afford him a hearing (*Corso v. Creighton University*, 1984).

THE RISK OF FACULTY HANDLING CASES ON THEIR OWN

The due process and contractually provided fair procedures are often ignored by faculty who prefer to confront students on their own (Jendrek, 1989; Lipson & McGavern, 1993). McCabe (1993) reported that on average more than half the faculty he surveyed said they ". . . would go to little or very little effort to document an incident" (p. 343). When faculty fail to document instances of academic dishonesty, they are risking serious problems for themselves and the community. Ignoring the problem only exacerbates the situation. Students are quick to recognize faculty indifference to academic dishonesty and see that as the diminution of the values of honesty and integrity.

Gehring and Pavela (1994) enumerated several "substantial threats to the educational enterprise" (pp. 6-7) brought about by widespread academic dishonesty. In addition to the ethical and community problems generated when faculty ignore cases of academic dishonesty, there are legal risks to faculty when they confront student cheating but ignore the process and handle cases of academic dishonesty on their own. As outlined above faculty at private institutions risk a breach of contract suit that could result in the court reinstating a student (*Corso v. Creighton University*, 1984). If the student has suffered an actual loss (e.g., not being able to practice a chosen profession, or having to repeat a semester and pay additional tuition) because of being given an F for cheating by a professor who chose not to follow the published process, then the student could also bring a tort suit for money damages against both the professor and the institution. Since the professor would have been acting outside the scope of employment by failing to follow university policy, the institution would likely not provide the professor with legal representation.

Faculty at public institutions are at even greater risk of suit if they do not follow the due process procedures outlined in institutional policies. Students' attorneys are very familiar with Section 1983 of Title 42 of the United States Code which provides:

> Every person, who, under color of any statute, ordinance, regulation, custom, or usage, of any State or Territory, subjects or causes to be subjected, any citizen of the United Sates or other person within the jurisdiction thereof to the deprivation of any rights, privileges, or immunities secured by the Constitution and laws, shall be liable to the party injured in an action at law, suite in equity, or other proper proceeding for redress.

This means that faculty at public institutions of higher education ("persons acting under color of state law") who act on their own without providing due process ("subjects . . . any citizen . . . to the deprivation of any rights . . . secured by the Constitution") may be sued personally for money damages ("shall be liable to the party injured in an action at law, suit in equity or other proper proceeding for redress"). Since failing to follow procedures contained in official publications would be acting outside the scope of one's employment the institution would not be obliged to provide legal representation. In addition any damages would be paid by the individual and not the institution.

MYTHS ASSOCIATED WITH REPORTING ACADEMIC DISHONESTY

There appear to be several reasons why faculty fail to report instances of academic dishonesty. A colleague once reported to the author that he did not charge a student in his class with cheating because it was just his word against the student's. Although one person's word against another's is not a strong case, hearing boards may find violations of academic integrity policies based solely on one person's word. In a case in which a student alleged that a professor granted him a waiver of a required course and the professor stated that he did not do so, the Supreme Court of Montana set forth criteria for evaluating evidence when one person's word is posited against another's (*Holloway v. University of Montana,* 1978). The court said:

> statements may be so inherently improbable the Court is induced to disregard them. Testimony may be contradicted by other facts. There may be so many omissions in the testimony that the witness' whole story is discredited. The witness' manner of testifying, his appearance and demeanor may be considered. Attendant circumstances may cast suspicion upon the narration of a particular event. Finally, the interest of any witness in the result of the trial or any bias he might have may properly be considered (p. 1267).

The court went on to note that because it found against the student's direct testimony did not necessarily mean his testimony was false. Rather, "It may be as easily assumed that, in light of the weight of other evidence against the testimony of Holloway, that Holloway could have been mistaken or he may have misunderstood the tenor or meaning of what Dr. Kempner told him" (p. 1269). While this case deals with a course waiver, it could be applied to a whole variety of academic dishonesty situations such as misunderstandings about help on homework assignments, take-home exams, papers, and lab assignments among others.

A New York court was faced with a case involving a student who claimed that he left an exam for only 10 or 15 minutes to obtain a calculator, while the professor alleged that he left with an exam and never returned until the end of the exam. The Hearing Committee found the student guilty of cheating on the exam and the student brought suit alleging insufficient evidence. The court observed that "as it is arguable that room for choice exists between the conflicting testimony, the respondent's [college's] decision as to which version of events to accept should not be disturbed" (*Abrahamian v. City University of New York,* 1991, p. 512). Thus, even when it is the faculty member's word against that of the student, faculty may go forward with allegations of cheating, and hearing boards may find students responsible.

Another apparent reason that causes faculty to fail to document and report cheating is their fear of being sued for defamation if the student is found not guilty. This is an unfounded fear. Gehring and Pavela (1994) reported that they have ". . . monitored and reviewed the pertinent case law related to academic integrity in higher education for over 30 years and have yet to find even one case in which administrators, faculty, or students have been assessed damages for reporting alleged acts of academic dishonesty" (p. 16).

Defamation is a false statement (libel if written and slander if spoken) made by one person to another about a third party which diminished that party's reputation in the community. A common defense against a charge of defamation is a "qualified privilege." A federal court of appeals noted that "It is well accepted that officers and faculty members of educational organizations enjoy a qualified privilege to discuss the qualifications and character of fellow officers and faculty members if the matter communicated is pertinent to the functioning of the educational institution" (*Greenya v. George Washington University,* 1975, p. 563). This privilege also extends to students who report others for acts of academic dishonesty. A qualified or conditional privilege would apply when: "(1) some interest of the person who publishes defamatory matter is involved; (2) some interest of the person to whom the matter is published or some other third person is involved; or (3) a recognized interest of the public is involved" [footnotes omitted] (*Vargo v. Hunt,* 1990, p. 627). In a situation where one student reported another to the proper authorities and was subsequently sued for defamation by the accused student, the court held that the student who reported the alleged offense enjoyed a conditional privilege. The court pointed out:

> Surely, as noted by the lower court, "the integrity of the academic process of the College" was an interest that impacted upon the students, faculty and administration alike, and this interest merited preservation through the "self-policing" eye of students in reporting "perceived" violations of the Honor code. Accordingly, the College community had a "common interest" in continuing a policy of "honesty" in the classroom, lest its reputation for "integrity" and graduating students possessing academic excellence and honesty be undermined in the public and private sector. And the Defendant's report to the Honor Committee of what she "perceived" the Plaintiff doing while taking an examination was merely a fulfillment of her "obligation" under the same Honor Code the Plaintiff agreed to uphold upon admission to Allegheny College (*Vargo v. Hunt,* 1990, p. 628).

Although this case involved an honor code, a similar finding of a conditional privilege would also apply where there was no honor code but simply a policy prohibiting acts of academic dishonesty.

While the conditional privilege is a defense against defamation, where a report is made to the proper officials, if an unreasonable degree of publication (either oral or written) is given to the accusation, the privilege may be lost. Likewise, where publication of the matter is made with malicious intent there would be no privilege. A faculty member told the campus police investigating a theft that he believed a student, Michael Bow, was responsible for the theft; however, he also made these remarks to a number of others not involved in the investigation and there was thus no "common interest." The student sued the faculty member for defamation and the faculty member claimed a conditional privilege. The Georgia Supreme Court held that the statements were made to persons not connected with the investigation and were malicious. The verdict of $200,000 against the professor was upheld (*Melton v. Bow,* 1978). The lesson of this case is to report acts of academic dishonesty to the proper authority and not to discuss the matter with anyone else not involved in the adjudication of the matter.

CONCLUSIONS

Gehring and Pavela (1994) provided a set of guidelines to protect academic integrity which is helpful in maintaining academic integrity on campus. The general themes they advance are important to both academic administrators and student affairs practitioners. Protecting academic integrity on campus is too important to be left only to academic affairs or only to student affairs. Both organizations need to cooperate to eliminate this pernicious problem. Student affairs administrators have a long history of learning about due process and the procedures to follow in cases of misconduct. This knowledge could be valuable in training faculty and hearing boards, whether the responsibility for adjudicating offenses is assigned to the academic or the student affairs personnel. No matter where the responsibility lies, the essence of due process must be maintained and student affairs administrators should be called on to lend their expertise in this area.

Most faculty do not realize the legal risks they assume when they handle acts of academic dishonesty without following institutional procedures. They must be educated to understand the necessity of the process and the process itself. Due process is not a mystical concept nor does it put them on trial. Faculty need to understand the concept and the process and have the myths debunked. Anything less is intentionally placing the faculty at risk. Even private institutions that are not required to conform to the Constitution should not have a problem with providing a reasonable notice and an opportunity for students to defend themselves. Faculty at these institutions no less must be aware of their obligations to conform to the contract. Educating faculty is not an easy task and must be approached creatively and with their contributions. Any effort to assist faculty in knowing how to prevent and confront acts of academic dishonesty will be appreciated, albeit with some grumbling along the way.

All these efforts should heighten the awareness and sensitivity of faculty and students to academic integrity on campus. Developing this awareness will not reflect negatively on the institution, rather it will communicate that the institution is serious about and highly values academic integrity.

References

Abrahamian v. City University of New York, 565 N.Y.S. 2d 511 (A.D. 1 Dept 1991).
Babcock v. New Orleans Baptist, 554 So. 2d 90 (La. App 4th Cir. 1989).
Boehm v. University of Pennsylvania School of Veterinary Medicine, 573 A. 2d 575 (Pa. Supp. 1990).
Boyer, E.L. (1990). *Campus life.* Princeton, N.J.: Princeton University Press.
Clayton v. Trustees of Princeton University, 608 F. Supp. 413 (D.C. N.J. 1985).

Collison, M. (1990a October 24). Survey at Rutgers suggests that cheating may be on the rise at large universities. *The Chronicle of Higher Education*, pp. A31-32.

Collison, M. (1990b January 17). Apparent rise in students' cheating has college officials worried. *The Chronicle of Higher Education,* p. A31.

Corso v. Creighton University, 731 F. 2d 529 (8th Cir. 1984).

Davidson v. New Orleans, 96 U.S. 97 (1877).

Dixon v. Alabama, 249 F. 2d 150 (5th Cir. 1961).

Esteban v. Central Missouri State College, 277 F. Supp. 649 (W.D. Mo., S.D. 1967).

Garshnau v. The Pennsylvania State University, 395 F. Supp. 912 (M.D. Pa. 1975).

General Order on Judicial Standards of Procedure and Substance in Review of Student Discipline in Tax Supported Institutions of Higher Education, 45 FRD 133 (W. D. Mo. 1968).

Gehring, D. (1993). Understanding the legal constraints on practice. In M. Barr (Ed.), *The handbook of student affairs administration.* San Francisco: Jossey-Bass, Inc.

Gehring, D., and Pavela, G. (1994). *Issues and perspectives on academic integrity* (2nd ed.). Washington, D.C.

Greenya v. George Washington University, 512 F. 2d 556 (D. C. Cir. 1975).

Harvey v. Palmer College, 363 N. W. 2d 443 (Iowa 1984).

Hill v. Trustees of Indiana University, 537 F. 2d 248 (7th Cir. 1976).

Henson v. Honor Committee of U. Va., 719 F. 2d 69 (4th Cir. 1983).

Holloway v. University of Montana, 582 P. 2d 1265 (Mont. 1978).

Jackson v. Hayakawa, 761 F. 2d 525 (9th Cir. 1985).

James v. Wall, 783 S.W. 2d 615 (Tex. App. 1989).

Jendrek, M.P. (1989). Faculty reactions to academic dishonesty. *Journal of College Student Development, 30,* 401-406.

Jones v. Board of Governors of the University of North Carolina, 704 F. 2d 713 (4th Cir. 1983).

Kalinsky v. State University of New York, 557 N. Y. S. 2d 577 (A.D. 3 Dept 1990).

Lexington Theological Seminary v. Vance, 596 S. W. 2d 11 (Ky. App. 1979).

Lightsey v. King, 567 F. Supp. 645 (E. D. N. Y. 1983).

Lipson, A., and McGavern, N. (1993). *Undergraduate academic dishonesty at MIT: Results of a study of undergraduates, faculty and graduate teaching assistants* (MIT Colloquium Committee, Undergraduate Academic Affairs).

Mary M. v. Clark, 473 N. Y. S. 2d 843 (A. D. 3 Dept. 1984).
McCabe, D.L. (1993). Academic integrity: What the latest research shows. *Synthesis: Law and Policy in Higher Education, 5,* 340-343.
McCabe, D.L., and Trevino, L.K. (1993). Academic dishonesty: Honor codes and other contextual influences. *The Journal of Higher Education, 64,* 522-538.
McDonald v. Board of Trustees of the University of Illinois, 375 F. Supp. 95 104 (N. D. Ill., E. D.).
Melton v. Bow, 247 S.E. 2d 100 (Ga. 1978).
Napolitano v. The Trustees of Princeton University, 453 A 2d 263 (N. J. Sup. 1982).
Olsson v. Board of Higher Education, 426 N. Y. S. 2d 248 (1980).
Pavela, G. (1988). "Legal issues." In W.L. Kibler, E.M. Nuss, B.G. Paterson, and G. Pavela (Eds.), *Academic integrity and student development: Legal issues and policy perspectives* (pp. 37-63). Asheville, NC: College Administration Publications, Inc.
Roberts v. Knowlton, 377 F. Supp. 1381 (S. D. N. Y. 1974).
Scott v. Alabama, 300 F. Supp. 163 (M. D. Ala. N. D. 1969).
Shelly v. Kraemer, 92 L. Ed. 1161 (1947).
Slaughter v. Brigham Young University, 514 F. 2d 622 (10th Cir. 1975).
Sohmer v. Kinnard, 535 F. Supp. 50 (D. Md. 1982).
State v. Hyman, 171 S.W. 2d 822 (Tenn. 1942).
Steinberg v. Chicago Medical College, 341 N. E. 2d 634 (Ill. 1977).
Stoner, E.N., and Cerminara, K.L. (1990). Harnessing the "spirit of insubordination": A model student disciplinary code. *Journal of College and University Law, 17*(2), 89-121.
University of Texas Medical School at Houston v. Than, 874 S.W. 2d 839 (Tex. App. 1994).
Vargo v. Hunt, 581 A. 2d 625 (Pa. Supp. 1990).
Wellborn, S.N. (1980, October 20). Cheating in college becomes an epidemic. *U.S. News & World Report,* pp. 39-42.
White v. Knowlton, 361 F. Supp. 445 (S. D. N. Y. 1973).
Wisconsin v. Constantineau, 400 U. S. 433 (1971).
Wright v. Texas Southern University, 392 F. 2d 728 (5th Cir. 1968).

7

THE EFFECT OF INSTITUTIONAL POLICIES AND PROCEDURES ON ACADEMIC INTEGRITY

Donald L. McCabe
Gary M. Pavela

Much of the available research on academic dishonesty suggests that institutional response to incidents of cheating tends to be reactive. Is it possible to create institutional policies and actions that are effective preventive means to address the problem? In this chapter, McCabe and Pavela provide a review of academic integrity from an institutional perspective and cite an example of a proactive approach to the issues related to academic dishonesty.

"The quality of education would dramatically increase if more effort was devoted toward ensuring that people don't cheat. Many people feel that those who cheat get better grades and better jobs with less effort because they cheat. Such lax rules keep the system extremely unfair."

These sentiments, as expressed by a student at a major state university on the west coast, capture the feelings of many college students. And for many, the failure of their college or university to maintain a system of fair and equitable competition in the classroom seems to be the only justification they need to rationalize their own cheating. Indeed recent surveys of cheating among college students suggest that the failure of most colleges and universities to develop a shared understanding and acceptance of their academic integrity policies among students has a significant and substantive impact on self-reported cheating (e.g., McCabe & Trevino, 1993). As McCabe and Trevino have argued, a 'cheating culture' develops on every campus that can be a powerful influence on students, and institutional strategies designed to shape and nurture this culture appear to be a critical element in controlling student cheating.

This chapter will review some of the strategies different schools have developed to enhance academic integrity among students. The components of these strategies that seem to make a real difference with students will be discussed, along with possible reasons for why they make a difference. Although several strategies will be presented, the modified honor code recently implemented at the University of Maryland at College Park will be highlighted as one example of a strategy that could be successful on many campuses.

THE PREVALENCE OF CHEATING

Student cheating has long occupied the attention of researchers and an extensive literature has developed that clearly documents the prevalence of cheating among college students. In spite of sometimes wide variations in research methodologies, survey instruments, and samples, most studies have found that half or more of college students have engaged in some form of academic cheating.

A landmark study in this research stream was conducted by Bowers (1964) over 30 years ago. Bowers' survey included over 5,000 students at 99 different schools across the country and examined a variety of cheating behaviors associated with both written work and examinations. Not only did Bowers show that cheating among college students was prevalent (over 75 percent of the students surveyed by Bowers admitted to at least one incident of cheating while in college), he also offered compelling evidence for the view that the strategy employed by an individual college or university could make a significant difference in the level of cheating found among students on its campus. For example, Bowers showed that schools that employed academic honor codes had significantly lower rates of self-reported student cheating.

McCabe and Trevino (1993) also conducted a large, multi-school study of student cheating and reported results very similar to those of Bowers.

Relying on a sample of over 6,000 students (primarily juniors and seniors) at 31 schools, McCabe and Trevino found a 67 percent incidence of self-reported cheating among their respondents. Like Bowers, they found significant variations in cheating among students on different campuses and concluded that honor codes and other contextual influences provided a major explanation for these differences.

Although generally more limited in scope, other studies of student cheating are numerous and have reported levels of cheating ranging from 13 percent to 95 percent (Collison, 1990; Eve & Bromley, 1981; Haines, Diekhoff, LaBeff & Clark, 1986; Harp & Taietz, 1966; Jendrek, 1989; Leming, 1980; Liska, 1978; Tittle & Rowe, 1973).

While many of these studies assume that cheating among college students has increased dramatically over the last 20 to 30 years, the empirical evidence for this view is mixed.

For example, McCabe and Bowers (1994) reported a comparative study of cheating among males in college in the 1960s and 1990s and concluded that, "trends in college cheating have remained remarkably consistent over the last 30 years. Although some changes are apparent, [our] data clearly argue against the position that student cheating in the 1980s and 1990s has escalated in dramatic fashion" (p. 5). In fact, the only substantive increase in cheating McCabe and Bowers found in this study was "a dramatic rise among all students in instances of unpermitted collaboration on written assignments" (p. 9). Some of their other comparisons actually suggested there has been a modest decline in the level of cheating among college students — particularly on written work. A major limitation of this comparison, however, was the fact that the sample was limited to students at relatively small, highly selective schools.

A more recent study by McCabe and Trevino (1996) suggested that not only does more cheating occur at moderately selective, larger state institutions, those that now educate the vast majority of the nation's college students, but cheating at these schools has increased significantly in the last 30 years. Working with nine medium to large state universities, which had participated in the original Bowers (1964) study, McCabe and Trevino (1996) found modest but statistically significant increases in both test cheating and cheating on written work. They observed a dramatic increase in instances of unpermitted collaboration on written work, but they also found significant increases in the number of students reporting they had either copied from another student during a test or exam or had helped someone else cheat on a test or exam in some way. Although student cheating on written work seemed to be comparable between this sample and students at the more selective schools in the original McCabe and Trevino (1993) sample that did not have honor codes, the level of test and exam cheating at the larger schools was significantly higher. Collison (1990) suggested that cheating may be higher at larger schools due in part to generally larger class sizes, a greater percentage of first-generation college students, and inadequate institutional strategies concerning academic integrity.

WHO CHEATS?

A major focus of research on student cheating has been an effort to understand individual differences thought to be predictive of cheating behaviors. For example, Ward and Beck (1990) reported that not only do male college students cheat more than female students but also that women who engage in cheating behaviors require "the psychological mechanism of excuse making more than men [in order] to engage in dishonest behavior" (p. 338). Baird (1980) also found that men tend to cheat more than women and that they were less likely to do anything when confronted with a friend they saw cheating. However, Stern and Havlicek (1986) found only modest differences in the cheating behaviors of men and women.

Both Baird (1980) and Hetherington and Feldman (1964) suggested that there is a significant direct relation between cheating and a student's grade point average. Eisenberger and Shank (1985) reported that "individuals with a high work ethic resisted cheating much longer on an unsolvable task than did those with a low work ethic" (p. 525). Perry, Kane, Bernesser, and Spicker (1990) demonstrated that students who exhibit Type A patterns of behavior, often characterized by competitive achievement striving, are more likely to cheat, particularly "in situations in which their expectations for success cannot be reached by exerting additional effort" (p. 463).

INSTITUTIONAL CONTEXT

Other studies have concentrated on the institutional level of analysis and examined contextual factors that seem to influence student cheating. In a study comparing the effectiveness of moral appeals and sanction threats on student cheating, Tittle and Rowe (1973) concluded that the threat of sanction had "a clear and substantial impact" (p. 488). Although Stern and

Havlicek (1986) found faculty to be generally more optimistic than students about the impact changes in the environment might have on student cheating, both groups did suggest that such factors as closer proctoring, smaller classes, the use of multiple forms of a test or examination, and an increase in individual interactions between faculty and students would probably reduce academic misconduct among students. Not surprisingly, Michaels and Miethe (1989) demonstrated that students were more likely to engage in academic cheating when they perceived the likelihood of getting caught and/or the perceived severity of penalties for cheating to be low.

Studies of institutional context are generally of greatest interest to student affairs and other university administrators. As suggested by McCabe and Trevino (1993), "(A)lthough the individual differences approach helps to understand individuals' predispositions to cheat, the findings are not particularly useful to the university administrator searching for effective institutional responses to issues of academic dishonesty" (p. 524). It is these "contextual factors that may be associated with academic dishonesty and that are open to administrative influence" that are of greatest interest to those charged with the responsibility of enhancing the level of academic integrity among students.

Although it is not an exhaustive list, McCabe and Trevino (1993) focused on five major variables in their investigation of the relationship between contextual variables and student integrity — student honor codes, student perceptions of the cheating behaviors of other students on campus (the 'cheating culture'), the degree to which students understand and accept the institution's academic integrity policies, the likelihood that a student might be caught cheating, and the severity of penalties for those who are found guilty of cheating.

The central focus of the McCabe and Trevino (1993) study, however, was student honor codes. Although many schools around the country utilize strategies to address academic integrity which incorporate some element of honor, McCabe and Trevino's study looked at what might be called 'strong' honor codes. They classified as honor codes only those academic integrity policies that met at least two of the criteria proposed by Melendez (1985): student exams are not proctored, some form of written honor pledge is used, students are expected (in some cases required) to report instances of academic dishonesty of which they are aware (the 'non-toleration' clause), and a peer judiciary exists where students have a major voice (the majority of members, the chairmanship, or students have the authority to change the judiciary's constitution) and the "primary concern [of the judiciary] is the infraction of honor by students" (p. 10).

Although Campbell (1935) and Canning (1956) had previously reported lower levels of cheating among students governed by honor codes, Bowers (1964) was the first to demonstrate the positive influence of honor codes in a large, multi-campus study. After conducting a series of analyses that controlled for gender, school size, school selectivity, and other factors, Bowers (1964) concluded

> it would seem that the campus community can make substantial progress in solving its academic dishonesty by instituting student-centered arrangements of control like the honor system. The moral responsibility such a system places on the student body presumably restrains dishonesty by heightening both the individual student's own moral stance on cheating and the stance of his peers (p. 192).

Although the impact of honor codes was greatest at smaller schools, they had a positive influence in all contexts examined by Bowers.

McCabe and Trevino (1993) reached similar conclusions, but again the mere presence or absence of an honor code was not a completely satisfying explanation of the differences in student cheating observed across different campuses. Although honor codes appeared to be a major influence in reducing cheating among students, McCabe and Trevino concluded that a more significant influence was the student culture that developed on campus concerning the question of cheating — whether it was considered socially acceptable, whether students felt they had primary responsibility for controlling cheating or whether the faculty and/or administration did, what their peers thought about the issue, and how their peers behaved. An honor code did much to create a peer culture that viewed cheating as socially unacceptable, but it is possible to create such a culture in the absence of an honor code.

McCabe and Trevino (1993) argued that perhaps the most significant element of any strategy designed to create a positive peer culture on a campus is the ability to create a *shared* understanding and acceptance of the institution's policies on academic integrity among both faculty and students. An honor code seems to be one generally effective way to do this, but it is not the only way. Indeed, McCabe and Trevino pointed out that a school in their sample with one of the lowest rates of self-reported cheating among its students did not have an honor code. However:

> [it] is strongly committed to the concept of academic honor, making it a major topic of discussion in its student handbook and at orientation sessions for incoming students, where it goes to great lengths to ensure that its policy is understood and that academic honor is the obligation of every member of the campus community (McCabe & Trevino, 1993, p. 534).

In contrast, one of the honor code schools in their sample had one of the higher incidences of cheating. "However, students [at this school] reported a low level of understanding and acceptance of the school's policy," which seemed to be related to diminished efforts on the school's part "in communicating and implementing its code in recent years" (McCabe & Trevino, 1993, p. 534). Indeed, McCabe and Trevino underscored the importance of student understanding and acceptance of the institution's academic integrity policies when they concluded:

> ... an institution's ability to develop a shared understanding and acceptance of its academic integrity policies has a significant and substantive impact on student perceptions of their peers' behaviors, the most powerful influence on self-reported cheating. Striving for mutual understanding of these policies may be extremely important. Thus, programs aimed at distributing, explaining, and gaining student and faculty acceptance of academic integrity policies may be particularly useful (pp. 533-534).

Although an honor code is one mechanism that may accomplish this objective, it is not the only one. As suggested by Michaels and Miethe (1989), faculty statements in course syllabi about academic misconduct and its consequences and consistent reminders about the seriousness and consequences of academic misconduct may also be effective.

A committee of students, faculty, and administrators at Rutgers University recently published a short manual entitled *Promoting Academic Integrity: A User-Friendly Guide* (Fishbein, 1994), which discusses several possible strategies that might increase student understanding of the value of academic integrity and thus reduce cheating. Concerned about student perceptions of Rutgers as a "large, impersonal institution that cares little about their welfare," a concern shared by students at many schools, the authors of this guide believe that "increased and improved contact between faculty and students" is one key to creating an environment where cheating is unacceptable. They recommend more frequent office hours and faculty participation in residence hall programs as possible remedies, arguing that students are less likely to cheat if they respect their professors.

The Fishbein committee at Rutgers also highlighted the need for faculty to make clear to students what actually constitutes cheating. Every faculty member has probably encountered some form of academic dishonesty where the student was convinced that he or she had done nothing wrong. Being explicit about one's expectations for written assignments seems to be particularly important. Some students make it through college without ever learning what actually constitutes plagiarism. Faculty should not assume that someone else has explained the 'rules' to their students unless they are aware of explicit programs to do so that are in place. Some institutions might be well advised to spend less time informing students about how suspected cases of cheating will be processed and more on helping students understand what constitutes honest work. Although this may be a daunting task at some large institutions, perhaps it should be considered a required element of a college education.

Although effective strategies for addressing academic dishonesty will be significantly influenced by an institution's unique context, there are some general guiding principles that should be helpful to all institutions. Fundamental among these are student involvement in developing and implementing academic integrity policies and appropriate involvement of faculty.

WHY STUDENT INVOLVEMENT IS NEEDED

Three converging trends seem to be prompting college administrators and student leaders to seek greater student involvement in promoting academic integrity:
- the apparent unwillingness of substantial numbers of faculty members to report cases of academic dishonesty;
- growing careerism among students, combined with a distrust of government and social institutions;
- a search by many students for moral leadership, and a willingness to work for the common good, if asked.

In a spring 1993 interview in *Synthesis: Law and Policy in Higher Education,* McCabe reported that his 1990 academic dishonesty survey revealed that 60 percent of the faculty at nonhonor code schools and 47 percent of the faculty at schools with honor codes "said they would go to little or very little effort to document an incident" of academic dishonesty (McCabe, 1993, p. 343).

Many factors account for faculty indifference to academic dishonesty — including an emphasis on research and publication rather than teaching; fear of confrontation and litigation; and the bad experiences some faculty members have had with burdensome university procedures. Another possibility, rarely discussed, may be uncertainty among faculty members about whether traditional values and virtues should be affirmed in the classroom at all. This was an issue raised by Clark University philosophy professor Christina Hoff Sommers (1993):

> Some time ago I published an article called "Ethics without Virtue," in which I criticized the way ethics is being taught in American colleges. I pointed out that there is an overemphasis on social policy questions, with little or no attention being paid to private morality . . .
>
> A colleague of mine did not like what I said. She told me that in her classroom she would continue to focus on issues of social injustice . . . She made it clear that I was wasting time and even doing harm by promoting bourgeois virtues instead of awakening the social conscience of my students.
>
> At the end of the semester, she came to my office carrying a stack of exams and looking very upset.
>
> "What's wrong?" I asked.
>
> "They cheated on their social justice take-home finals. They plagiarized!" More than half the students in her ethics class had copied long passages from the secondary literature. "What are you going to do?" I asked her. She gave me a self-mocking smile and said, "I'd like to borrow a copy of that article you wrote on ethics without virtue" (pp. 3-4).

Faculty members who seek to instill a sense of social obligation without affirming personal virtues are planting trees without roots. Those who refrain from discussing the importance of academic integrity, or look the other way when students engage in academic dishonesty, alienate honest students and foster a climate of moral cynicism on campus.

A campus climate of moral cynicism can also be fostered when large numbers of students view their education primarily as a means to gain competitive advantage in an uncertain economy, governed by social institutions they do not trust. Recent national surveys show that substantial majorities of students see career preparation as the primary purpose of a college education (National Association of College Admissions Counselors, 1994). There is also evidence that many high-achieving young people are "ever more distraught with the society in which they are coming of age" and evidence a "steep decline" in confidence in the government (Sanchez, 1995, p. A3).

The cynicism such unchallenged perspectives can breed was reflected in an interview conducted by Gary Pavela with a University of Maryland at College Park student being expelled for academic dishonesty:

Q. "Is [engaging in cheating] fair to [honest] students?"
A. "I don't think of it like that. I know some students do. But the

attitude is generally, this is the way it is. When they work, a lot of these kids, either their fathers work in business, whatever they do, they get a shortcut — the other guy doesn't. That's the way I look at it. If I'm sharp enough to know the right people to get what I need, and he's not, then that's the point of the whole thing."

Yet there is more to the current generation of young people than discouraging survey data suggest. Many seek ethical guidance and are capable of making "harsh moral judgments about themselves" (Chira, 1994, p. 1). Others feel a sense of obligation to the larger society, manifested in a strong commitment to community service. For example, Independent Sector, a nonprofit coalition of corporate, foundation, and voluntary organizations, reported in 1994 that 61 percent of teenagers surveyed in 1991 were involved in volunteer activities, averaging 3.2 hours a week. The most frequently cited reason for volunteering, identified by 59 percent of the volunteering teens, was a belief that "it was important to help others." Independent Sector found that the critical factor inducing most teens to volunteer was simply being *asked* to volunteer (Knauft, 1994).

THE MARYLAND MODEL

Asking students to exercise moral judgment, and to work for the common good, are essential components of a "modified" honor code (the "Code of Academic Integrity") adopted by the University of Maryland at College Park in 1990. The Maryland approach is rooted in the belief that the careerism and cynicism associated with the current generation of students derives not from any intrinsic shortcoming in American youth, but from a failure on the part of adults to give young people opportunities to test and develop their character.

Although it is not a panacea, the Maryland model has been attracting increasing attention from student affairs administrators around the country. The model not only centers on increased student involvement, but it provides a well thought-out staged implementation strategy. The major elements of the Maryland academic integrity program include:

■ *Involving students in educating their peers and resolving academic dishonesty allegations.* Recent national surveys show a high rate of cheating in secondary schools. A 1995 survey conducted by the publication *Who's Who Among American High School Students* found, for example, that the proportion of "high achieving" high school students who reported that they have "cheated to get ahead academically" increased from 70 percent in 1983 to 78 percent in 1995 (cited in Sanchez, 1995, p. A3). Given what appears to be widespread acceptance of academic dishonesty in high schools, it is essential for higher education institutions to enlist the one force most likely to influence student values: the student peer group. At Maryland, this means giving a 40-person Student Honor Council the following responsibilities:

    a. educating students and faculty members about university academic integrity policies and procedures;

    b. affirming the importance of academic integrity in regular communications to newly admitted students, students enrolled in introductory courses, and in other forms of campus-wide programming. Student Honor Council programming in 1995 included a free showing of the film "Quiz Show," preceded by a widely publicized panel presentation on ethics in government and education;

    c. encouraging the reporting of academic dishonesty and receiving academic dishonesty allegations from any source;

    d. constituting the majority on "honor review" hearing panels created to hear contested allegations of academic dishonesty;

    e. exercising exclusive authority to impose (and remove) the "X" portion of the "XF" grade penalty, coded on the official transcript as "failure due to academic dishonesty." The XF is designated as the "standard" penalty for academic dishonesty at Maryland. It must remain on the transcript for a minimum of one year. The "X" portion of the "XF" can only be removed by first-time offenders who complete a six-week, noncredit "academic integrity seminar."

■ *Treating academic integrity as a moral issue.* The fact that students are valued and entrusted with responsibility for challenging their peers to adhere to a higher standard for academic integrity increases the likelihood that the standard will be seen as legitimate by the student body as a whole. There is good evidence in this regard that the perceived moral legitimacy of the law is essential to its effective enforcement. For example, Tyler (1990) drew upon a study of a random sample of 1,500 Chicago residents to conclude what proponents of honor codes have argued for years:

> In trying to understand why people follow the law . . . we should not assume that behavior responds primarily to reward and punishment . . . Instead, we should recognize that behavior is affected by the legitimacy of legal authorities and the morality of the law. Similarly, the literature on implementing policy should not focus simply on manipulating penalties and incentives: *it should also be concerned*

with creating a normative climate that promotes the acceptance of law and public policies (emphasis added) (pp. 168-169).

In addition to educating their peers, members of the Student Honor Council at Maryland also enhance their own moral development. Student Honor Council members are some of the university's most promising students. By serving on the council (e.g. making presentations, adjudicating cases, formulating policies) they practice the essence of Aristotle's (1962) ethics:

> For all the things which we have to learn before we can do them, we learn by doing: men become builders by building houses and harpists by playing the harp; similarly we become just by the practice of just acts, self-controlled by exercising self control . . . Hence it is no small matter whether one habit or another is inculcated in us from early childhood; on the contrary, it makes a considerable difference, or, rather, *all* the difference (p. 34).

University of Maryland Student Honor Council members also promote ethical dialogue by encouraging faculty members to see academic dishonesty from a moral perspective. Student Honor Council correspondence to the faculty in 1994, for example, asked teachers and teaching assistants to stress in classroom discussions that it is morally wrong for students to gain an unfair advantage over others by cheating.

Finally, a moral perspective is also enhanced on campus when proceduralism is reduced. The Maryland *Code of Academic Integrity* provides for prompt, informal resolution of uncontested cases and for fair but streamlined hearings when students assert their innocence. Courtroom procedures, legal representation, a "beyond a reasonable doubt" standard of proof, and appeals to other committees or boards are not allowed (unless expulsion or suspension is contemplated). The desired tone of hearings is specified in the Maryland *Code of Academic Integrity* as follows:

> The basic tenets of scholarship — full and willing disclosure, accuracy of statement, and intellectual integrity in hypothesis, in argument and in conclusion — must always take precedence over the temptation to gain the particular resolution of the case. An Honor Review is not in the character of a civil or criminal proceeding. It is not molded on these adversarial systems; nor does it serve the same social functions. It is not a court or tribunal. Rather it is an academic process unique to the community of scholars that comprise a university.

■ *Promoting enhanced student-faculty contact and better teaching.* Gehring and Pavela (1994) observed that "academic dishonesty is far less likely to occur in small classes where there is a significant, positive relationship between students and teachers." One of the most important missions of the Maryland Student Honor Council is to encourage teaching styles and examinations that call for active student participation, frequent interaction with faculty members, and critical thinking rather than memorization. For example, in regular Student Honor Council correspondence to faculty members, faculty members are advised that they are less likely to encounter plagiarism and purchased papers if they use frequent, in-class writing assignments, ask for regular progress reports from students, and couple longer term paper assignments with oral presentations. Also, faculty members are urged to consider techniques such as allowing students to take notes on a 3-by-5-inch card, and to use the card during examinations. This practice encourages students to organize and think about what they have learned, and reduces the likelihood that "crib" sheets will be used.

The University of Maryland *Code of Academic Integrity* has been in operation for five years. Two years ago the code successfully passed a review by the Campus Senate. All indications — from the willingness of faculty members and students to report cases, to the level of student involvement on the Student Honor Council — have exceeded expectations. Under its former "administrative" academic integrity system, the university processed 60-90 allegations of academic dishonesty a year. Now, nearly twice that number of cases are resolved. The primary reasons for the increased number of cases are better reporting and broader acceptance of university academic integrity policies. Further evidence of the code's acceptance has been a decision by the university's academic honors program to encourage faculty members to administer unproctored examinations for students who agree to sign an honor pledge.

CONCLUSIONS

Although the benefits may be hard to quantify, strategies such as the Maryland *Code of Academic Integrity* commit the university to a simple but critical process: the deliberate effort to discuss and affirm some of the basic ethical precepts underlying the academic enterprise. An effort to affirm such precepts was once a core mission both of secular and religious institutions of higher education. Careful initiatives designed to revitalize the best aspects of that mission will be of lasting value not only to faculty members and administrators, but also to students seeking ethical guidance and looking for ethical commitment.

Research suggests positive peer cultures on campus lead to reduced levels of student cheating. We believe such initiatives are the critical ingredient in developing these positive peer cultures. The success of such initiatives at the University of Maryland and other schools suggests students are willing to accept these responsibilities when properly motivated and challenged to do so.

References

Aristotle. (Ostwald trans.) (1962). *Nicomachean ethics.* New York: Macmillan.

Baird, J.S. (1980). Current trends in college cheating. *Psychology in Schools, 17,* 512-522.

Bowers, W.J. (1964). *Student dishonesty and its control in college.* New York: Bureau of Applied Social Research, Columbia University.

Campbell, W.G. (1935). *A comparative study of students under an honor system and a proctor system in the same university.* Los Angeles: University of Southern California Press.

Canning, R. (1956). Does an honor system reduce classroom cheating? An experimental answer. *Journal of Experimental Education, 24,* 291-296.

Chira, S. (1994, July 10). Worry and distrust of adults beset teenagers, poll says. *New York Times,* p. 1.

Collison, M. (1990, October 24). Survey at Rutgers suggests that cheating may be on the rise at large universities. *The Chronicle of Higher Education,* pp. A31-A32.

Eisenberger, R., and Shank, D.M. (1985). Personal work ethic and effort training affect cheating. *Journal of Personality and Social Psychology 49,* 520-528.

Eve, R.A., and Bromley, D.G. (1981). Scholastic dishonesty among college undergraduates: Parallel tests of two sociological explanations. *Youth and Society, 13,* 3-22.

Fishbein, L. (Ed.). (1994). *Promoting academic integrity: A user-friendly guide.* Unpublished guide prepared by the Provost's Committee to Promote Academic Integrity, Rutgers University, New Brunswick, NJ.

Gehring, D., and Pavela, G. (1994). *Issues and perspectives on academic integrity.* Washington, D.C.: National Association of Student Personnel Administrators.

Haines, V., Diekhoff, G., LaBeff, E., and R. Clark. (1986). College cheating: Immaturity, lack of commitment, and the neutralizing attitude. *Research in Higher Education, 25,* 342-354.

Harp, J., and Taietz, P. (1966). Academic integrity and social structure: A study of cheating among college students. *Social Problems, 13,* 365-373.

Hetherington, E.M., and Feldman, S.E. (1964). College cheating as a function of subject and situational variables. *Journal of Educational Psychology, 55,* 212-218.

Jendrek, M.P. (1989). Faculty reactions to academic dishonesty. *Journal of College Student Development, 30,* 401-406.

Knauft, E.B. (1994). *America's teenagers as volunteers.* Washington, D.C.: Independent Sector.

Leming, J.S. (1980). Cheating behavior, subject variables, and components of the internal-external scale under high and low risk conditions. *Journal of Educational Research, 74,* 83-87.

Liska, A. (1978). Deviant involvement, associations and attitudes: Specifying the underlying causal structures. *Sociology and Social Research, 63,* 73-88.

Melendez, B. (1985). *Honor code study.* Cambridge, Mass.: Harvard University.

McCabe, D.L. (1993). Academic integrity: what the latest research shows. *Synthesis: Law and Policy in Higher Education, 5,* 340-343.

McCabe, D.L., and Bowers, W.J. (1994). Academic dishonesty among males in college: A thirty year perspective. *Journal of College Student Development, 35,* 5-10.

McCabe, D.L., and Trevino, L.K. (1993). "Academic dishonesty: Honor codes and other contextual influences." *Journal of Higher Education, 64* (5), 522-538.

McCabe, D.L., and Trevino, L.K. (1996). What we know about cheating in college: Longitudinal Trends and Recent Developments. *Change, 28,* 28-33.

Michaels, J.W., and Miethe, T. (1989). Applying theories of deviance to academic cheating. *Social Science Quarterly, 70,* 870-885.

National Association of College Admissions Counselors, 1994. The class of '94: Where they stand. *Careers and Colleges Magazine,* 1-8.

Perry, A., Kane, K., Bernesser, K., and Spicker, P. (1990). Type A behavior, competitive achievement-striving, and cheating among college students. *Psychological Reports, 66,* 459-465.

Sanchez, R. (1995, June 15). Survey finds maturity, cynicism among high-achieving teens. *Washington Post,* p. A3.

Sommers, C.H. (1993). Teaching the virtues. *The Public Interest, 111,* 3-13.

Stern, E.B., and Havlicek, L. (1986). Academic misconduct: Results of faculty and undergraduate student surveys. *Journal of Allied Health, 15,* 129-142.

Tittle, C.R., and Rowe, A.R. (1973). Moral appeal, sanction threat, and deviance: An experimental test. *Social Problems, 20,* 488-497.

Tyler, T. (1990). *Why people obey the law.* New Haven: Yale University Press.

Ward, D.A., and Beck, W.L. (1990). Gender and dishonesty. *The Journal of Social Psychology, 130,* 333-339.

ACADEMIC INTEGRITY AND CAMPUS CLIMATE AT SMALL COLLEGES

KAREN O. CLIFFORD

Academic integrity has been the focus of numerous studies over the past 60 years. Most documented academic integrity studies have focused on large universities. This chapter presents the findings from a recent study examining students' perceptions of academic integrity at small colleges.

Academic dishonesty among college students is a widespread and serious problem for American higher education, as concluded by numerous reports in the professional literature as well as the popular press (Aaron & Georgia, 1994; Carnegie Council, 1979; Gordon, 1990; Haines, Diekhoff, LaBeff & Clark, 1986; Maramark & Maline, 1993; Singhal, 1982). Further, research by McCabe and Trevino (1996) revealed that more cheating occurs at moderately selective, larger state institutions, which enroll the majority of college students in this country. Despite the disturbing cheating statistics presented by these reports (and others referred to in Chapter 4), there is a common perception that there is less cheating at small colleges, where smaller classes and campuses contribute to students knowing one another and knowing their instructors.

IS THERE LESS CHEATING AT SMALL COLLEGES?

Several studies have examined the relationship between size of institution and cheating (Centra, 1970; Bowers, 1964; Goldsen, Rosenberg, Williams & Suchman, 1960; Davis, Grover, Becker & McGregor, 1992), and only one of these (Centra, 1970) considered the relationship between type of institution (e.g., public, private, church-sponsored, single-sex, military) and cheating. Bowers (1964) and Goldsen et al. (1960) found that colleges with higher cheating rates tend to be large. Bowers determined that there are higher cheating rates at colleges and universities that are coeducational and not highly selective in their admission requirements.

In studies of over 8,000 students at a variety of schools from disparate locations in the United States, Davis et al. (1992) found that the percentages of men and women at small, private liberal arts colleges who reported having cheated in college were significantly lower than those reported by their counterparts at larger state and private institutions. Similarly, in a 1993 survey of over 6,000 students at 31 selective colleges and universities, McCabe found that students at larger universities are more likely to engage in academic dishonesty than their counterparts at smaller institutions (McCabe & Trevino, 1993).

In two samples of entering freshmen from 119 institutions, Centra (1970) found that those institutions enrolling students with strong attitudes against cheating were generally more selective, all-female, and small in size. Centra's sample excluded institutions at which a student honor code exists. With respect to cheating attitudes by type of college, Centra reported that the eight Catholic men's colleges had the highest percentage of students with lenient responses. He attributed these lenient cheating attitudes in part to the fact that seven of these eight Catholic men's colleges had lower admissions requirements and to the fact that they were all-male colleges. Previous research had indicated that women reported lower cheating rates than men (Hetherington & Feldman, 1964).

Graham, Monday, O'Brien, and Steffen (1994) surveyed 480 students from two small colleges (a private Catholic college and a community college) in the Midwest to examine student and faculty perceptions of cheating at small liberal arts colleges. While there was not total agreement on what behaviors constituted cheating, nearly 90 percent of these students reported that they had engaged in some form of cheating at least once. In contrast to the previous research on cheating among students at small colleges (Centra, 1970; Davis et al., 1992; and McCabe & Trevino, 1993), Graham et al. (1994) found that cheating does appear to be as much a problem on small campuses as on large campuses. They concluded that

> it may be easier to control situations on smaller campuses with smaller class sizes. The strongest influence on cheating appears to be attitudes and norms about cheating. Small colleges should work on developing an environment in which cheating is not tolerated. This can be done through making the schools views about cheating clear. Institutions should also work on encouraging students to explore their own attitudes toward cheating in an effort to help students clarify how they feel (1994, p. 260).

CAMPUS CLIMATE AND ACADEMIC INTEGRITY

Centra's (1970) study raised the question of whether the incidence of cheating at different types of colleges is related entirely to the types of students who enroll or whether there are climates at some institutions that discourage cheating. Similarly, Graham et al. (1994) suggested that small colleges should work on developing environments in which cheating is not tolerated. Are there environments or campus climates that discourage cheating? Are these environments characteristic of small colleges? If there are campus environments or climates that discourage cheating and foster academic integrity, what are the elements of such a campus environment? The Center for Academic Integrity (CAI), a national organization comprised of students, faculty, and administrators from more than 70 colleges and universities in the United States, Mexico, and Canada, has identified the following list of key elements or institutional characteristics that they believe are necessary in creating a campus environment that fosters academic integrity:

- an atmosphere of trust and mutual respect between students and faculty
- a sense of community and absence of anonymity
- a shared responsibility among students, faculty, and administration for maintaining the institution's standards regarding academic integrity
- open, risk-free communication between faculty and students
- a sense of pride and inclusion in a shared collective mission or common purpose
- clarity and articulation of institutional values and priorities

- rituals and symbols that convey the importance of academic integrity and serve as mechanisms for passing on traditions
- student participation in making and enforcing rules
- support for academic integrity from all levels of the campus community
- clear expression and regular discussion of expectations for academic integrity and the reasons why it is valued
- the support for and benefits of academic integrity outweigh the burden of enforcement
- integration of the academic and social aspects of campus life (CAI, 1992).

While the center believes that these elements of campus climate promote academic integrity at colleges and universities, regardless of enrollment size or other characteristics, there is considerable agreement that these elements seem to most accurately characterize small, private colleges.

No research has examined the extent to which the elements listed above or others reported in the literature are actually present or being created by colleges and universities; however, Clifford (1996) surveyed 1,013 students from 17 small colleges in a study sponsored by the Center for Academic Integrity to examine students' perceptions of these elements. Specifically, this study surveyed students' perceptions of whether these and other components of campus climate promote academic integrity; whether the elements exist on their campuses; and the relationship between their perceptions of their campus climate and their self-reported incidence of cheating.

METHODOLOGY OF THE STUDY

For the purpose of this study, "small colleges" were defined as 4-year, liberal arts colleges with full-time undergraduate enrollments of 5,000 or less. A sample of 40 institutions was selected from the 1994 Carnegie Classification of Institutions of Higher Education, which "includes all colleges and universities in the United States that are degree-granting and accredited by an agency recognized by the U.S. Secretary of Education" (Carnegie Foundation, 1994, p. ixx). The institutions in the study were selected from Baccalaureate (Liberal Arts) Colleges I, which includes institutions that are primarily undergraduate colleges with major emphasis on baccalaureate degree programs, restrictive in admissions, and award 40 percent or more of the baccalaureate degrees in liberal arts fields, and from Baccalaureate Colleges II, which have the same characteristics as Baccalaureate Colleges I with the exception that they are less restrictive in admissions. Thus, the results of this research may be generalized to small colleges with enrollments of 5,000 or less which have been classified as Baccalaureate I or Baccalaureate II by the Carnegie Foundation. A stratified random sample was utilized, which included representation from each of the four subgroups of the population (Baccalaureate I and Baccalaureate II, public and private). A total of 17 institutions from 14 different states throughout the United States participated in the study. Nine institutions were private, and 8 institutions were public. Surveys were administered to groups of predominately non-freshman students in courses with a cross-section of majors, and a total of 1,013 usable surveys were collected.

Instrument

The survey instrument, identified as the "Student Attitude Survey," was developed by the researcher for this study. The survey was based on the elements of campus climate identified by the Center for Academic Integrity and encompassed several additional factors that are administrative devices for the prevention of cheating recommended in the professional literature. These factors included: proctoring during exams (Houston, 1976; Singhal & Johnson, 1983), alternate seating arrangements (Mueller, 1953), alternate exam forms, avoiding the use of past exams and paper topics (Barnett & Dalton, 1981), severe penalties for those caught cheating (Tom & Borin, 1988), and publishing the outcomes of academic dishonesty cases in the campus media (Aaron, 1992).

DEMOGRAPHIC RESULTS

Surveys were administered to groups of predominately non-freshman students in courses with a cross-section of majors, and a total of 1,013 usable surveys were collected. The percentages of male and female respondents were 48 percent and 52 percent, respectively. Ages ranged from 17 to 53, with the mean age at 22.5 years. The respondents were primarily upperclassmen, comprised of 27.1 percent sophomores, 31.8 percent juniors, 37.1 percent seniors, 2.3 percent freshmen, and 1.7 percent graduates. Only 11.7 percent of the respondents were members of fraternities or sororities. Almost 45 percent of the respondents planned to attend graduate or professional school upon graduation. Most of the respondents indicated that they had grade point averages of 2.0 or above: specifically, 23 percent reported a 3.5 or higher; 35 percent reported a 3.0-3.99; 40.6 percent reported a 2.0-2.99; and 1.3 percent reported a 1.99 or below. When asked to rate the competitiveness for grades on their campuses, 10.1 percent of the respondents answered "very high," 56.6 percent answered "high," .9 percent added in their own category of "medium," 29.9 percent answered "low," and 2.1 percent answered "very low." The respondents represented 16 categories of undergraduate majors, as well as a small number (.1 percent) of students completing postgraduate studies.

Approximately 80 percent of the respondents indicated that their campuses have a written policy or code of conduct for academic honesty. Less than 1 percent reported that their campuses do not have such a policy, while 19 percent indicated that they did not know. Almost 45 percent of the respondents indicated that their institutions have honor codes, while approximately 7 percent indicated that their institutions do not have honor codes and over 48 percent did not know. In contrast to the self-reported data, it was determined by the researcher through contact with the survey administrators that 16.2 percent of the respondents actually were enrolled at institutions with honor codes, while 86.3 percent of the respondents were at institutions with an institutional policy or code of conduct for academic honesty and 13.7 percent of the respondents were at institutions with no campus-wide policy or code of conduct governing academic honesty.

STUDENTS' PERCEPTIONS OF THE EXISTENCE OF THE ELEMENTS OF CAMPUS CLIMATE ON THEIR CAMPUSES

A majority of students strongly agreed or agreed that most of the elements of campus climate listed on the "Student Attitude Survey," particularly those identified by the Center for Academic Integrity, described their campuses. The elements specifically related to communication of their institutions' academic dishonesty policies received the highest agreement from students in describing their campuses. For example, over 81 percent of student respondents agreed that there is explicit communication that academic dishonesty is unacceptable and will not be tolerated on their campuses. Almost 71 percent agreed that there is explicit, clear communication of exactly what behaviors constitute academic dishonesty. There was less agreement with several other items pertaining to the means for this communication, however. Fewer than 33 percent of the respondents agreed that faculty members discuss the reasons why students should not cheat. Approximately 34 percent agreed that their college's stance on academic dishonesty is addressed as a major topic at orientation; and about 10 percent agreed that the results of specific cases of cheating are published in the campus media.

The elements of campus climate pertaining to faculty-student interaction were also reported by most students as being present on their campuses. Over 83 percent of the student respondents agreed that faculty members promote respect and personal involvement in the classroom by knowing students' names, establishing personal trust, and reducing students' feelings of anonymity on their campuses. Almost 75 percent agreed that there is open, risk-free communication between faculty and students. Similarly, over 77 percent indicated that faculty members on their campuses are enthusiastic and care about teaching.

There were several important elements that received less agreement from students in describing their campuses. While other studies have concluded that one of the most important determinants of the amount of cheating on college campuses is the level of disapproval of cheating among a students' college peers (Bowers, 1964; McCabe & Trevino, 1993), fewer than half of the student respondents in this study agreed that cheating is socially unacceptable among students on their campuses. Less than 37 percent of the respondents indicated that there is peer support on their campuses for academic honesty (for not cheating and for not helping others cheat).

The elements that students least agreed described their campuses were the administrative deterrents to cheating identified in the professional literature. Approximately 40 percent of the student respondents agreed that faculty members on their campuses use different tests/exams for different class sections, while less than 39 percent agreed that faculty members make cheating difficult by using alternate seating and/or test forms. Finally, only 25.6 percent agreed that faculty members on their campuses do not use past exams, tests, assignments, or topics for papers.

IMPORTANCE OF THE ELEMENTS OF CAMPUS CLIMATE IN PREVENTING CHEATING

Most students indicated that nearly all of the elements of campus climate listed on the "Student Attitude Survey," particularly those identified by the

Center for Academic Integrity, were important to them personally in preventing cheating and promoting the value of academic integrity.

The students in this study clearly indicated that faculty-student interaction is most important to them in preventing cheating and promoting academic integrity. Almost 96 percent of the student respondents indicated that it is important to them that faculty members are enthusiastic and care about teaching (65 percent of the students indicated that this element is "extremely important" to them). Likewise, approximately 97 percent responded that it is important to them that faculty members promote respect and personal involvement in the classroom by knowing students' names, establishing personal trust, and reducing students' feelings of anonymity (63 percent indicated that this element is 'extremely important' to them). Over 96 percent of the respondents reported that it is important to them that there is open, risk-free communication between faculty and students. Finally, 94.5 percent indicated that it is important to them that faculty members are sensitive to the academic pressure and exam/test stress that students face.

The elements students found less important involved external deterrents or interventions such as faculty members using different tests/exams for different class sections; avoiding the use of past exams, tests, assignments, or topics for papers; and placing students in every other seat or row and/or changing the order of test questions.

FACTORS INFLUENCING STUDENTS' DECISION TO CHEAT OR NOT TO CHEAT

Students were asked in the survey through an open-ended question to indicate what factors influence their decision to cheat or not. The most frequently cited reasons for not cheating were: personal morals, self-respect, integrity, and honesty; and risks, penalties, and consequences of getting caught. Other reasons for not cheating included: the need to learn the material for the "real world," job, MCATs, LSATs, and other entrance exams; honor code; guilt; parents' disapproval or upbringing; religious beliefs; peer pressure not to cheat; respect for professor; and unfairness to others. When the responses of students from institutions with honor codes were examined separately, a majority of these responses indicated the importance of the honor code in preventing cheating. For example, some typical responses from students at honor code institutions included: "Personal honor is more important than personal gain. It's not something that someone can tell you to do. It has to come from within yourself."; "My honor and the right thing to do" and "Honor above self." Similarly, many responses from students at church-sponsored institutions reflected their religious beliefs and values. Some examples of typical responses from students at church-sponsored institutions were: "My Christian faith — I believe it is wrong to cheat"; "obedience to God and his Word"; "spiritual conviction"; and "God is watching."

The most frequently cited reasons for cheating were very consistent with the commentary from the student focus groups of Kaplan and Mable in Chapter 2 and included: the need for and importance of getting good grades and fear of failing, and time, stress, and workload factors, including amount of studying. Other reasons for cheating were: difficulty and/or fairness of course material; whether other students are cheating; importance of course or assignment; and need for help with homework. Many students indicated that they cheated due to poor instruction and/or lack of respect for faculty members. Examples of such responses included: "the teacher is mean"; "lame teachers who do not clearly state what to study"; "how fair or unfair the teacher is;" "the instructor's attitude and approach to the class"; "if the teacher is too lazy to make up new questions, then I have the right to cheat." One student explained, "If I feel unjustly taught and feel that I've been ignored by the professor, then I feel as for their lack of responsibility to teach more clearly that I will use cheating as the final resort." Similarly, many students blamed their cheating on how easy it is to cheat and on whether or not other students are cheating. Examples of such responses included: "whether the teacher is 'dumb' enough not to notice people cheating"; "vision of the teacher and size of class"; "does the teacher watch closely and does your neighbor sit very close with the same test."

RELATIONSHIP BETWEEN SELF-REPORTED CHEATING AND PERCEPTIONS OF CAMPUS CLIMATE

To determine whether there was a relationship between self-reported incidence of cheating and students' perceptions of the elements of campus climate that prevent cheating, a cheating index was developed by combining the survey questions that asked students to report their incidence of cheating during the last academic year. Four questions at the end of the "Student Attitude Survey" specifically asked students to report whether they had cheated on a daily assignment or quiz (treated as "minor cheating") or on a major exam or assignment (treated as "major cheating") and how often. Correlations were calculated between the cheating index and students' perceptions of each of the elements of campus climate

Significant negative correlations were found between self-reported cheating and students' perceptions of their campuses for 26 of the 31 elements at the .05 significance level. The negative correlation indicates that as the cheating index increases (i.e., more cheating reported), the students' perceptions that the elements of campus climate are present decreases. The five variables that were not significantly related to cheating were: proctored exams, alternate seating/test questions, faculty members asking students not to cheat, alternate test forms for different class sections, and integration of academic and social aspects of campus life.

Analysis of students' perceptions of the importance of these elements of campus climate to them personally resulted in relationships between the cheating index and most of the elements. The variables that were not significantly related to cheating were: proctored exams; alternate seating/test questions; faculty members asking students not to cheat, alternate test forms for different class sections; integration of academic and social aspects of campus life; faculty members discuss the reasons why students should not cheat and create opportunities to explore the ethical dilemmas created by cheating; faculty members do not use past exams, tests, or paper topics; faculty members are enthusiastic and care about teaching and about their students; faculty members are sensitive to the academic pressure and exam/test stress that students face; and assignments/exams are fair and not too demanding.

EXTENT OF SELF-REPORTED CHEATING

The purpose of this study was not to determine the extent of cheating among students at small colleges; however, questions concerning the extent of cheating were addressed in order to obtain the correlations between students' perceptions of the elements of campus climate and their self-reported incidence of cheating. Approximately 35 percent of the students in this study indicated that they had cheated during the last 12 months. Almost 33 percent of the students reported that they had engaged in cheating on a daily assignment or quiz, while roughly 2 percent admitted to engaging in cheating on a major exam or assignment. These cheating rates were lower than those reported by many studies, which is consistent with the studies that have found less cheating at small colleges. Given the fact that these percentages refer to cheating that students reported engaging in during the last academic year (rather than during their entire college career), it is possible that the percentages of cheating reported in this study underestimate the overall amount of cheating. Since a specific definition of cheating was not provided on the survey instrument, it is also possible that these percentages are underestimated as a result of students' uncertainty of what behaviors actually constitute cheating.

ANALYSIS AND CONCLUSIONS

The findings of this study indicate clearly that students at small colleges agreed that most of the elements of campus climate listed on the survey instrument were important to them in preventing cheating and that, overall, the elements identified by the Center for Academic Integrity were more important to them than the cheating interventions. Most students further agreed that many of these elements were present on their campuses, which affirms that most of these elements characterize small colleges. The significant correlations that were found between students' self-reported cheating and their perceptions of the elements of campus climate are further evidence of the importance of these elements in preventing cheating. These correlations confirmed that there is an inverse relationship between students' self-reported cheating and their perceptions that these elements are present on their campuses. Nearly all of the elements that did not have significant correlations with cheating were administrative roadblocks or deterrents to cheating identified in the professional literature, such as the proctoring of exams and tests, placing students in every other seat or row, changing the order of test questions, and using different tests/exams for different class sections.

Students' responses to the open-ended question concerning factors that influence their decision to cheat or not were consistent with the research that has concluded that cheating depends upon the situation. The reasons most frequently listed for cheating were the need for or importance of a good grade and workload factors and/or the amount of studying. Students cited reasons for *not* cheating far more frequently than reasons *for* cheating, however, and the most frequently cited reasons for not cheating were personal morals and/or integrity and the risks or consequences of getting caught.

The students in this study identified the elements relating to the relationship between faculty and students and classroom atmosphere as the most important elements in preventing academic dishonesty and promoting academic integrity. Many students confirmed the importance of the classroom atmosphere and the relationship between faculty and students by reporting that lack of respect for professors, inadequate instruction, and lack of attention to cheating were factors that influenced their decision to cheat.

Finally, most of the students in this study also indicated that peer support for academic honesty is important to them in preventing them from cheating, which is consistent with the finding of previous research that the strongest influence on cheating appears to be the attitudes and behaviors of students' peers (McCabe &Trevino, 1993).

RECOMMENDATIONS

There is no single answer for promoting academic integrity on all college campuses, because each institution has its own unique mission, values, traditions, and student and faculty characteristics. However, based on the findings and conclusions from this study, the following recommendations can be made to higher education institutions, regardless of their size:

- Institutions should find ways to create campus climates that promote academic integrity. This study confirmed students' perceptions of the importance of the key elements or institutional characteristics identified by the National Center for Academic Integrity in creating such a campus environment. Institutions should establish and promote these elements in a manner consistent with their mission, values, traditions, and faculty and student characteristics.
- Institutions must find comprehensive methods for communicating to their students that academic integrity is an important value, that academic dishonesty is unacceptable and will not be tolerated, and that all members of the campus community must be responsible for promoting academic integrity. The importance of academic honesty must be communicated as soon as students arrive on campus, and there must be explicit, clear communication of exactly what behaviors constitute academic dishonesty. This communication must be ongoing and should include notification of the outcomes of actual incidents of academic dishonesty in a manner that protects the

confidentiality of the students involved. Institutions should also consider establishing symbols, ceremonies, and traditions that are unique to their campuses that communicate that academic integrity is an important value.

■ Institutions should pay particular attention to classroom atmosphere and the relationship between faculty and students. Students affirmed in this study that the elements of campus climate relating to the relationship between faculty and students and classroom atmosphere were the most important elements to them in preventing academic dishonesty and promoting academic integrity. They reported that inadequate instruction, unfair grading methods, lack of respect for professors, and faculty indifference to cheating were factors that influence their decision to cheat. Thus, institutions should recognize and reward faculty members who are enthusiastic and care about teaching, who invite and encourage open communication with students, and who promote respect and personal involvement in the classroom.

■ Institutions should involve students in the development and enforcement of rules concerning academic dishonesty in order to increase their understanding of the reasons for these rules and to encourage them to accept greater responsibility for implementing the rules. Almost 80 percent of the students in this study indicated that students' participation in making rules and enforcing them was important in preventing them from cheating.

■ Institutions should find ways to recognize and reward students' personal honesty, integrity, and accomplishment and to recognize and help students deal with the pressure for grades. Institutions should reexamine their missions and priorities to determine whether the level of competitiveness for grades among their students is appropriate or excessive.

■ Institutions should find ways to foster peer support for not cheating. Honor codes are the most recognized strategies for creating campus climates where there is peer support for not cheating and where academic dishonesty is socially unacceptable. Honor codes provide a means for communicating the values and expectations of the institution, for establishing an environment of trust, and for giving students responsibility for dealing with issues of academic dishonesty. Even though only 3 of the 17 institutions in this study had honor codes, the findings support previous research that has concluded that lower levels of cheating have been found where the primary responsibility for academic honesty has been given to students through honor codes. Many of the students from the three honor code institutions in this study reported that the honor codes at their institutions prevented them from cheating.

References

Aaron, R.M. (1992). Student academic dishonesty: Are collegiate institutions addressing the issue? *NASPA Journal, 29,* 107-113.

Aaron, R.M., and Georgia, R.T. (1994). Administrator perceptions of student academic dishonesty in collegiate institutions. *NASPA Journal, 31,* 83-91.

Barnett, D.C., and Dalton, J.C. (1981). Why college students cheat. *Journal of College Student Personnel, 22,* 545-551.

Bowers, W.J. (1964) *Student dishonesty and its control in college.* New York: Bureau of Applied Social Research.

Carnegie Council on Policies in Higher Education. (1979). *Fair practices in higher education: Rights and responsibilities of students and their colleges in a period of intensified competition for enrollment.* San Francisco: Jossey-Bass, Inc.

Carnegie Foundation for the Advancement of Teaching. (1994). *A classification of institutions of higher education.* Princeton, N.J.: author.

Center for Academic Integrity (CAI). (1992, March 5-7). Unpublished proceedings from first annual conference, Rutgers, NJ.

Centra, J.A. (1970). College freshman attitudes toward cheating. *Personnel and Guidance Journal, 48,* 366-373.

Clifford, K. (1996). College students' perceptions of academic integrity and campus climate at small colleges (Doctoral dissertation, University of Virginia, 1996).

Davis, S.F., Grover, C.A., Becker, A.H., and McGregor, L.N. (1992). Academic dishonesty: Prevalence, determinants, techniques, and punishments. *Teaching of Psychology, 19,* 16-20.

Goldsen, R.K., Rosenberg, M., William, R., and Suchman, E. (1960). *What college students think.* New York: D. Van Nostrand.

Gordon, L. (1990, November 22). Study finds cheating joins 3 Rs as a basic college skill. *Los Angeles Times,* p. A5.

Graham, M., Monday, J., O'Brien, K., and Steffen, S. (1994). Cheating at small colleges: An examination of student and faculty attitudes and behaviors. *Journal of College Student Development, 35,* 255-260.

Haines, V.J., Diekhoff, G.M., LaBeff, E.E., and Clark, R.E. (1986). College cheating: Immaturity, lack of commitment, and the neutralizing attitude. *Research in Higher Education, 25,* 342-354.

Hetherington, E.M., and Feldman, S.E. (1964). College cheating as a function of subject and situational variables. *Journal of Educational Psychology, 55,* 212-218.

Houston, J.P. (1976). The assessment and prevention of answer copying on undergraduate multiple-choice examinations. *Research in Higher Education, 5,* 301-311.

Maramark, S., and Maline, M.B. (1993). *Academic dishonesty among college students.* Washington, D.C.: U.S. Dept. of Education, Office of Educational Research and Improvement.

McCabe, D.L., and Trevino, L.K. (1993). "Academic dishonesty: Honor codes and other contextual influences." *Journal of Higher Education, 64* (5), 522-538.

Mueller, K.H. (1953). Can cheating be killed? *Personnel and Guidance Journal, 31,* 465-468.

Singhal, A.C. (1982). Factors in students' dishonesty. *Psychological Reports, 51,* 775-80.

Singhal, A.C., and Johnson, P. (1983). How to halt student dishonesty. *College Student Journal, 17,* 13-19.

Tom, G., and Borin, N. (1988). Cheating in academe. *Journal of Education for Business, 63,* 153-157.

9

CAN THE ACADEMIC INTEGRITY OF COST-EFFECTIVE DISTANCE LEARNING COURSE OFFERINGS BE PROTECTED?

Mary Elisabeth Randall

One of the fastest growing segments of our student communities is "distance learners." Students who are distance learners rarely come to their institution's traditional campus, nor do they attend class in the traditional classroom. How can we manage academic integrity for classrooms without the traditional faculty-student interface? This chapter suggests that many of the same elements that determine the prevalence of cheating in the traditional classroom work in similar ways for the distance learner.

What is Distance Education?

Distance education is simply defined as a form of education in which learner and instructor are separate during a majority of the instruction. Shifting demographics (fewer traditional students and more adult learners), declining economic support for education, competing public policy agendas, and probing questions about the relevance and worth of existing curricula, degrees, and pedagogy have led to difficult times on campuses across the country. Distance education is one way in which access can be provided without the cost of building and maintaining the traditional bricks and mortar. Unlike independent or self-directed study, distance education usually infers the presence of an institution that plans complete degree programs and provides supporting resources and services for its students.

The emergence of powerful and pervasive electronic technologies has opened the door to new roles for colleges. The era of educational monopolies is ending. By the beginning of the next century, people who were historically placebound and educationally isolated will be served by an expanding number of institutions using informational technologies and modern telecommunications. These will include but not be limited to broadcast television, microwave, direct broadcast satellite, cable television, and the Internet.

This changing technological capacity to serve learners wherever they live or work is raising new questions about the need for differentiating roles between and among institutions. The new technologies have led distance learners and their instructors into new possibilities for interaction and information access. Adults find distance education, with its savings in commuting time, an easier fit into their busy lives. Adults are comfortable, too, with the independent structure of the distant classroom and are more likely to possess the self-motivation to focus on educational goals away from a campus setting.

Equipped with the new technologies, universities and colleges have greater opportunities for individualized instruction, as communication between student and instructor changes in such a way that they may never come in direct contact with one another. Distance education, then, becomes as inclusive or personal as the individual and instructor elect. The Maine Bureau of Labor's 1986 statistics indicated that less than one-third of adults in Maine lived within a 12-mile radius of one of the University of Maine System's seven institutions. For generations, in many states such as Maine and Nebraska, barriers of geography, cost, and time have restricted people who live in rural communities from participating in higher education. New technological systems provide unique educational structures and powerful new technologies for citizens of all ages, regardless of where they live.

The new electronic infrastructures, when used effectively, shrink barriers of time and distance, bringing these new educational opportunities to isolated, rural communities at a time when their contributions to a literate, well-trained citizenry are essential to states' economic well-being. Various technologies such as interactive television, computer conferencing, telephone bridging, compressed video, and the Internet are some that are in use today.

DIFFERENCES BETWEEN
TRADITIONAL AND DISTANT LEARNING SITES

No research could be found that compares the prevalence of cheating in the traditional classroom and that which occurs in the distance education learning environment. It can be assumed, however, that academic dishonesty does occur and must be confronted. Although codes of student conduct must be promulgated and enforced for distance learners, a preventive mechanism that should be communicated to all faculty who teach in the distance learning classroom is to humanize, as much as possible, the seemingly detached learning process associated with distance learning.

At the distant site there is not necessarily an opportunity for students to interact with the instructor before and after class. Thus, other methods are developed to enhance communication. These methods include computer conferencing, electronic mail, toll-free telephone numbers for faculty, audio conferencing through the use of telephone bridges, and open time over the interactive system for routine academic/course advising. In most situations, the issues in the classroom that present problems are not unlike those on campuses with large lecture sections; they just are in more than one location. Some faculty are so adept at bridging the technological gap that the only difference between the traditional classroom and the distance locations, besides the presence of technology, is the geographic distance between the instructor and the student.

How do faculty humanize the student experience for distance learners?

Just as teaching techniques differ from one faculty member to another, those used in distance learning vary as well. Distance educators need to break from the traditional model of teaching to see interaction in broader terms. Creating an environment that offers security, quality, and openness from the first class session helps contribute to the course's climate, and as we have seen in previous chapters, a climate that is supportive to closer faculty-student interaction will reduce the likelihood of cheating. Establishing this climate is important but must be enhanced with structured experiences and accesses so *all* students will participate. Distance educators often provide more than a "talking head" for the television camera by showing slides, asking their academic support camera staff to vary angles, camera positions, and background scenes. All these enhancements assist the student to be a more active learner. Other suggested techniques are:

- ■ *photographs* — Some distance educators request that students send in photographs of themselves. When the student is participating over the audio link, the faculty member displays that student's photograph on the classroom camera so others in the class see what the student looks like.
- ■ *use of student names* — Faculty can code students' names by location and thus call on students at that location to encourage participation.
- ■ *site visits* — There are faculty who make it a point to visit each site of the course at least once during a semester to meet informally with students there. This is more difficult to do in classes with a large number of receive sites.
- ■ *informal preclass activities* — Faculty can offer open microphones before classes begin or just after they end, or they can offer open time different from the class time to encourage conversations, questions, or call-ins.
- ■ *call-in office hours* — Faculty can provide time exclusively for distance students who may call them in their offices.
- ■ *other methods* — There are other methods provided for out-of-classroom communication that may include voice mail, electronic mail, fax (facsimile), and computer conferencing.

Some faculty make it a point to elicit comments and questions from the distance sites by calling on a particular group to report to the entire class. There are classes that are team taught, where one of the faculty might be facilitating class while another is accepting calls for questions and feedback from other students in the class activity. Use of various technologies can ensure that all students can and will take an active part in their learning experience. While there are some faculty who continue to offer traditional lectures and make no specific attempt to personalize the experience for the student, this is not the recommended method of instruction.

HOW ACADEMIC QUALITY IS ASSURED

When asked why they cheat, one response often heard (see Chapters 2 and 10) is that the quality of a professor's teaching was inferior so "I cheated because the professor wasn't teaching me what I needed to know for the test."

To assure students academic quality in addition to access, the distance learning programs must assist faculty by:
- providing adequate teaching support, consistent and expert technical assistance, special training programs for use of new technology, adequate release time for course preparation, and increased financial remuneration;
- limiting faculty participation to those who seek to be involved, who by experience and background have demonstrated outstanding teaching ability, who have shown commitment to nontraditional learners, and who demonstrate a willingness to travel extensively;
- offering special recognition status and prestige with distant faculty assignments;
- encouraging faculty members to work with colleagues to assist each other in the refinement of their teaching skills;
- establishing a representative process that includes faculty in considering course scheduling, program development, faculty assignments, faculty support and development programs, and evaluation procedures; and
- developing a handbook for faculty that includes guidelines for instructional planning and delivery, faculty development opportunities, academic services, video production services, student support services, and helpful hints from those experienced teaching students at a distance.

Student support services are also mandatory to ensure students have opportunities to succeed. These services include:
- effective recruiting and admissions services, academic and career counseling, adequate financial aid, and other academic support services
- an enhanced sense of community for students who are far from a college campus; these may include special on-campus receptions for distant students, study group opportunities at the distant site, receptions for students and faculty at distant sites, and informal study areas where students may congregate
- resources and opportunities for human growth and development, including intellectual, cultural, vocational, emotional, philosophical, social, and physical development.

Studies have shown that students at a distance perform as well as those in the traditional classroom (Johnson, 1991b, 1991c; Holdampf, 1983). This may be, in part, linked to student motivation. In some classes it has been found that there are no significant differences in grades received, while in other classes the distant students performed better than those in the traditional classroom.

HOW FACULTY PROMOTE ACADEMIC INTEGRITY AMONG DISTANT LEARNERS

As in the traditional classrooms, faculty are aware of the need for academic integrity from their students. In September 1989, the University of Maine at Augusta began a statewide distance education program using an interactive television network. It offers six associate degrees and one baccalaureate degree through approximately 50 courses per semester. The interactive television network utilizes one-way video, two-way audio transmission, utilizing point-to-point microwave and fiber optic cable. The network is connected to the 7 campuses of the University of Maine System, the 6 technical colleges, the Maine Maritime Academy, 11 off-campus centers, and more than 60 of Maine's secondary schools (Johnson, 1991a).

Personal interviews were conducted with 10 full-time faculty who teach in the distance education program at the University of Maine at Augusta, and each indicated a belief that the distant learner has no greater inclination to cheat than does the traditional student. As with the traditional classroom, instructors should establish class expectations at the first class meeting. Faculty members may ask that other students present in the distance learning classroom inform him/her if the students observe any possible cheating behavior in their classroom. One faculty member's syllabus states "... Safeguarding the academic integrity of the course itself depends first upon the honesty and commitment of the students themselves. This is the first method of quality assurance. Please make the instructor aware of any and all events that detract from the academic quality of the course . . . enough supports are offered such that cheating should neither be needed nor profitable" (Elliott, 1995).

Many faculty members believe that students should be responsible for their own learning. These faculty members inform their students orally and in the course syllabus that academic honesty is their expectation of all students. They make it clear that it is a student's responsibility to assure class decorum and integrity. Some routinely, but randomly, ask for reports from distant locations on what the classroom climate is like. Although they may have only subjective data to reinforce their belief, some believe, perhaps naively, that the honor system works for the most part. Most, however, take seriously the challenge of designing the distant learning classroom experience to prevent cheating. The faculty who utilize the technology network believe that it provides some challenges that are different from those in the traditional classroom, but for the most part, it only exacerbates challenges and problems that pervade education. Their suggestions, many of which also apply to the traditional classroom, are listed below:

- *open book examinations* — Many shared their perception that students study less for an open-book examination.
- *take-home examinations* — Preparing exams in this format may reduce the need for cheating.
- *writing samples* — Several ask for frequent writing samples from students; require brief, oral reports and presentations to the class that provide opportunities for individual styles of students.
- *unique multiple-choice examinations* — These, just as when used in large lecture halls, provide little to no opportunity to look at the work of others.
- *alternate multiple choice examinations* — This is similar to the method above.
- *machine-scored examinations* — The answer sheets are difficult to overlook and copy precisely.
- *proctors* — They are required for all examinations.
- *less emphasis on examinations* — Several faculty no longer place major emphasis on examinations; they require in-class participation, oral reports, many written assignments, and group work. This appears to create less student anxiety and pressure regarding test performance. Faculty also report that these methods require more instructor review and correction time.
- *verification of examinations* — Proctors require identification of students to be provided when examinations are completed.
- *collection of examinations* — Tests are collected by proctors once they have been reviewed.
- *grading variations* — instructors look for variations in grading patterns of students.
- *class patterns* — Faculty review class performance at each site that might indicate cheating if all students received the same grade or missed the same examination questions.

- *perfection is suspect* — Seeing perfection once will cause some faculty to watch for a pattern.
- *peer review* — Students do oral presentation of written work, and it is reviewed by peers as part of the grade.
- *controlled makeup examinations* — The time and place of makeup examinations is tightly controlled, and the examination is different from the one given to the entire class.
- *established relationship with proctors* — The proctors may not be employees of the university delivering the course. Thus it is important for the faculty member to establish a relationship with the proctor, to discuss expectations from them, and to meet with them if possible.
- *more than one proctor* — Depending on the size of a class, it may be necessary to have more than one proctor.
- *no examinations at home* — If students are enrolled through a cable television connection in their homes, they must be required to attend a proctored site to take all take-home examinations.
- *students must know their rights* — Students should be provided with a copy of the institution's student conduct code. This should be done either by the instructor or as part of the institution's policy.

CONCLUSIONS

In summary, the faculty interviewed offered many suggestions on how to prevent cheating in the distance education classes but indicated that they see the problems as the same ones they face in their traditional classroom. Adults are motivated learners who enroll for classes that are convenient in time, place and cost (Brickell, 1995).

Learning is a very individual effort, particularly in distance education, and distance educators should plan activities that enhance student experiences and motivation (Verduin & Clark, 1991). Distance educators emphasize that the personalized experience for students is critical to successful teaching. Increased interaction with distant learners is most likely to result in involved, motivated students who experience little pressure to resort to academic dishonesty as a means to good grades.

References

Brickell, H. (1995). *Adults in the classroom.* New York: College Entrance Examination Board.

Elliott, K. (1995). *Introduction to Psychology 100 syllabus.* Augusta, Me.: University of Maine.

Holdampf, B. (1983). *Innovative associate degree nursing program — remote area.* Department of Occupational Education and Technology, Texas Education Agency (ED 248 402).

Johnson, J. (1991a, March). *Report on a study of the Community College of Maine interactive television system returning faculty fall 1990.* Portland, Me.: University of Southern Maine.

Johnson, J. (1991b, April). *A comparative study of the Community College of Maine interactive television system courses and live equivalent courses fall 1990.* Portland, Me.: University of Southern Maine.

Johnson, J. (1991c, October). *Evaluation report of the Community College of Maine interactive television system summer 1991.* Portland, Me.: University of Southern Maine.

Verduin, J., Jr. & Clark, T. (1991). *Distance education: The foundations of effective practice.* San Francisco: Jossey-Bass, Inc.

10

THE IMPACT OF TECHNOLOGY ON ACADEMIC INTEGRITY

HAROLD GOLDSMITH

The current technology explosion has had a revolutionary impact on higher education. How can higher education institutions be prepared for the repercussions of changing technology? What are the implications of rapidly changing, often esoteric technology in the monitoring of standards of academic integrity? In this chapter, Goldsmith provides a framework for understanding how technology will change our educational environment.

The impact of technological developments on college and university campuses is difficult to miss these days. Just a few years ago, campus technology as characterized by large mainframe computers and "homegrown" software were tightly controlled by a few computer specialists. The development of personal computers and the ability to link or network them together has placed computer power in the hands of individual users that the college or university cannot control.

The next wave of technological change is upon us. It is the computer network whose potential impact on teaching and learning is daunting. The network permits computer users to access a virtually limitless number of resources and to remotely retrieve information in a variety of formats.

Keller (1982) in *Academic Strategy* identified the technological imperative as one of the six shifts that will affect the future of higher education. Writing in the 1980s, Keller underestimated the impact that technology has and will have on higher education.

Perelman (1992) described technological developments in four broad categories: 1) the smart environment; 2) the telecosm; 3) hypermedia; and 4) brain technology.

The "smart" environment is an environment in which most products have some technological capability. Programmable calculators, video recorders that teach users how to program them, and tutorials built into computer software programs are examples of the "smart" environment (Perelman, 1992).

Telecosm is the term used to describe the networks that tie all the technology together. The World Wide Web and Gopher are very familiar to faculty and students on college campuses. Prodigy and CompuServe are examples of commercial services offering access to information resources and access to the Internet. These networks offer users unparalleled access to information resources only dimly imagined a few years ago (Perelman, 1992).

Hypermedia refers to the growing capability to manage, sort, and manipulate the exploding amount of software and information resources available. The "Windows" program is an example of hypermedia that simplifies the use of a computer.

Brain technology is a field that studies the brain as a chemical processing unit. These studies have resulted in developments in technology such as fuzzy logic and bubble memory (Perelman, 1992). Perelman suggested that future technological developments will fall into one of these four categories.

THE NEW TECHNOLOGIES

Burrus (1993) identified 24 new technologies that will transform the ways we live, learn, and work. For this discussion about academic integrity, the technologies of most relevance are:

■ *Electronic notepads.* Electronic notepads are hand-held computers. The user writes on them with an electronic pen. Many have memory. They do permit the exchange of information and most are wireless.

The Apple "Newton" is an example of this type of device.

■ *Multimedia computers*. Burrus (1993) described multimedia computers as combining the "audiovisual power of television, the publishing power of the printing press, and the interactive power of the computer." They permit the storage, retrieval, and display of information in many formats. Most major manufacturers are now marketing these computers.

■ *Advanced compact disks*. Advanced compact disks are new versions of the common audio compact disks. These disks can contain sound, data, and video that permit the user to interact with the program on the disk (Burrus, 1992). "Explorers of the World" (in Floyd, 1995b) is an example of this type of CD-Rom program.

■ *Advanced simulations.* Advanced simulations are software programs that allow a student to use the computer to do or experience activities or events such as flying, chemistry experiments, even surgery. The latest types of advanced simulation are "virtual reality" programs that allow users to "step into a virtual world" of sights, sounds, and touch (Burrus, 1993). The "Chemsite" program is "an interactive molecular building tool that allows users to build, display, and simulate the actions of chemical structures" (Floyd, 1995a).

■ *Advanced expert systems.* Advanced expert systems are software programs that take information about best practices in a field of interest and create decision matrices that give solutions to complex problems. Such programs can be applied to management, accounting, personal decision making, and training. (Burrus, 1992). The "Electronics Workbench" permits users to design and troubleshoot electronic circuits (Floyd, 1995b).

■ *Personal communication networks*. Personal communication networks are like cellular telephones but they are cheaper and static free (Burrus, 1993).

THE NEW TECHNOLOGY APPLIED TO
ACADEMIC DISHONESTY

These technological developments offer great promise to enhance teaching and learning, but they also offer opportunities for academic dishonesty. Technology can be misused to plagiarize, cheat, and receive unauthorized aid.

Plagiarism

By using the Internet, students now have access to world-wide information sources. Within a very short time, students will have access to virtual libraries that will permit the instant retrieval of sources. For instance, the University of Queensland announced that its database on microscopy and microanalysis is available through the World Wide Web (Floyd, 1995c). The announcement said that "biological abstracts, physical science abstracts, and images" are available. A biology professor who assigns a paper on microscopy will most likely know the resources available locally. Students who have access to the World Wide Web will, however, have international resources available to them.

These materials are instantly available to students. The ability of an instructor to identify sources is much more complex because of the potential of the use of world-wide resources to retrieve the information.

Cheating on Exams, Papers, or Projects

Students can cheat on examinations, papers, or projects using sophisticated technology. Programmable calculators allow students to put formulas in memory that may give students unfair advantage over students who do not use them.

Wireless personal communications — cellular telephones, electronic notepads, and wireless modems — permit students to communicate with, and receive information from, others not in the testing situation. This technology is no longer experimental. The University of California at Santa Cruz has recently installed a wireless modem network throughout the campus (DeLoughry, 1995). Other institutions are experimenting with this technology and private wireless services are offering new products.

Solutions' manuals or other instructor's aids can be placed on the Internet or retrieved remotely from other institutions and used for take-home or other exams. In addition, many universities are using help lines on the Internet where questions could be posted and answers received to help with take-home tests or projects.

Unauthorized Aid

Unauthorized aid includes the use of software, databases, or expert advice that is contrary to the wishes of the professor. Unauthorized aid might include software that checks spelling, punctuation, and grammar. Software is also now available that will instantly translate foreign languages either from English to the foreign language or from that foreign language into

English. Software is available that can help solve mathematical problems. The Internet provides many sources to get information about almost any topic. Students can pose questions and get advice from the network resources. In addition, as suggested earlier, the ability to reach and use remote data bases increases opportunities for unauthorized aid.

Recommendations
Student and academic affairs administrators responsible for academic integrity issues will need to become more aware and stay abreast of the rapidly changing technologies and their potential for use and abuse.

■ *Know what computer facilities are available on campus.* Because the use of technology is diffused through the campus, administrators and faculty must also be aware of all computer labs and their capabilities. In addition, administrators and faculty must be aware of network access capabilities available on campus or through commercial or free services operating in their area.

■ *Gain knowledge of software or network resources.* Software and new network capabilities are developing at a very rapid rate. To remain currently informed, administrators will need to peruse a variety of resources. One of the most helpful is the weekly section in the *Chronicle of Higher Education* dealing with technology. Library and computer center staff are also a rich source. The various Internet faculty discussion groups may also be a resource.

■ *Modify course and test designs to make cheating more difficult.* Faculty should assess course requirements and learning objectives in light of easy access to technological resources. Can in-class exercises, group work, project-based work, or other strategies be used to minimize cheating? When a faculty member wants a benchmark measure of content knowledge, can in-class writing assignments, pop quizzes, or other kinds of assignments substitute for out-of-class work? Can active learning strategies be used to minimize the misuse of technology?

■ *Use security programs for computer test materials and files.* Just as computer program software is becoming more sophisticated, so are the security programs that help prevent unauthorized use. Faculty members should regularly review the security procedures used for classes where students have computer accounts. They should change passwords frequently and immediately if passwords have been compromised. Data security and devices like passwords, should be one issue discussed with students at the beginning of class.

■ *Establish clear policies about the use of calculators and other aids during tests.* Faculty need to be much more explicit about the kinds of aids that can be used during tests. If students have programmable calculators, do they have to demonstrate that the memories are cleared before an exam? If students have electronic notepads, are these devices checked? To assume that students do not or cannot get access to certain kinds of technologies may not be realistic. Faculty members should state if they are limiting the electronic sources that can be used and identify the kinds of aids they will permit during a test.

■ *Establish clear policies about unauthorized aid, including the use of computer, CD-Rom or network resources.* Because students can access virtually limitless resource data bases, instructors should establish clear parameters for courses. If only local resources are to be used, the professor must specify this. If network "homework helper" resources are not to be used, the professor must make this clear. If CD-Rom or other software programs cannot be used in assignments, the professor should make this known. A faculty member can announce general course policies about the use of technology in the course syllabus.

■ *Establish clear policies about the use of electronic devices in test-taking situations.* Some students will argue that listening to music helps them relax during an exam, but much can come through headphones other than music. Students can record their crib notes and listen to them or students could conceivably have two-way communication with another student outside the testing environment. If laptop computers are permitted, is the use of a wireless modem prohibited? Are students permitted to have wireless telephones in the testing setting? Are electronic notepads permitted? Some answers may seem self-evident but faculty members can avoid any confusion by establishing and enforcing clear policies.

CONCLUSIONS

In their book, *Technology in Student Affairs,* Baier and Strong (1994) identified several administrative and ethical issues related to the growing use of technology. Academic dishonesty must be added to that list. Technological developments are redefining teaching and learning.

No administrator or faculty member can know all the possible ways for technology to be misused. Student and academic affairs staffs must collaborate to educate students about their ethical responsibilities involving the use of technology and to develop policies that permit early intervention when the misuse of technology is discovered.

Ultimately, regulation will not overcome the need to create a classroom culture that both celebrates the new opportunities that technology creates, while reducing its potential misuses.

References

Baier, J., and Strong, T. (1994). Technology in student affairs: Issues, applications, and trends. Lanham, Maryland: American College Personnel Association.

Burrus, J. (1993). Technotrends: How to use technology to go beyond your competition. New York: Harper Business.

DeLoughry, T. (1995, July 7). "No wires, an alternative to cabled computing passes a test at Santa Cruz." *The Chronicle of Higher Education,* pp. A15-16.

Floyd, B. (1995a, September 8) "Chemsite" in Information technology resources. *The Chronicle of Higher Education,* p. A32.

Floyd, B. (1995b, September 22). "Electronics workbench" in Information technology resources. *The Chronicle of Higher Education*, p. A36.

Floyd, B. (1995c, October 6). "University of Queensland" in Information technology resources. *The Chronicle of Higher Education,* p. A24.

Keller, G. (1982). *Academic strategy: The management revolution in American higher education.* Baltimore: The Johns Hopkins University Press.

Perelman, L.J. (1992). *School's out: Hyperlearning, the new technology, and the end of education.* New York: William Morrow and Company, Inc.

CONCLUSIONS

The authors of this monograph have addressed many of the critical issues related to the problem of academic dishonesty. Numerous interventions and strategies for addressing this growing problem in higher education have been suggested. Although individual chapters focused on aspects of this issue, many of their suggestions and conclusions have common themes which weave together to form a practical guide for faculty, administrators, and students in promoting academic integrity on their campuses.

The underlying theme of the monograph emphasized the need for colleges and universities to create a campus climate or culture that values and promotes academic integrity in every endeavor. Unfortunately, higher education is faced with the critical task of countering what McCabe and Pavela call the "cheating culture" of today's college students. To have an impact, colleges and universities must implement measures that will counter this firmly entrenched "cheating culture," which is eroding the academic foundations of our colleges and universities. To create a climate that values and promotes academic integrity requires an investment and commitment by all members of the institutional community. What is required is not simply the establishment of new rules for students and faculty to follow, but rather a thoughtful examination of ethical values and the meaning of integrity in the perspective of contemporary culture.

Collectively, the authors suggest that the starting point in creating such a climate lies in understanding the values systems and goals of contemporary college students and in developing interventions aimed at character building, teaching ethical values, peer accountability, and creating a learning environment that focuses less on competition and more on the process of learning. Just as important as educating students about academic integrity, colleges and universities must educate faculty about the impact they have on the students' perceptions of the learning environment, and the importance of consistent efforts to *promote* academic integrity and to *prevent* academic dishonesty.

A subsequent step in establishing a campus climate that values academic integrity is communicating institutional expectations to all members of the community. Certainly, students must be made aware of their responsibility as scholars. The authors point out that on many campuses this communication begins and ends with the publication of the disciplinary policy or honor code in the student handbook. Underlying this communication there must be a solid commitment to academic integrity which is manifest at every level of the institution. Institutions cannot afford to miss opportunities to educate faculty and students about academic integrity. What is required is a comprehensive effort to interact with students through many vehicles (classrooms, new student orientation, newspaper articles, campus programs) about the written policy, expectations, definitions of academic dishonesty, the adjudication processes, sanctions, and underlying institutional values.

The authors agree that the problem will not simply vanish. Academic dishonesty has been a part of higher education since its earliest days. Technology is quickly changing the learning environments. Campuses are no longer defined by buildings and grounds. As higher education embraces distance learning, virtual classrooms, and expanding computer technologies, we must realize that academic dishonesty will keep pace with evolving technology.

In addition to the topics covered in this monograph, there are some issues that merit further review and investigation. Hearing officers report a disturbing increase in the number of graduate students who are relying on academic dishonesty to help them complete advanced degree programs. This disturbing trend seems to suggest that if academically dishonest behaviors are not addressed effectively early in a student's educational career the behavior may continue in advanced degree program. Additionally, international student advisors report that international students are often accused of academic dishonesty violations because of differences in cultural mores. These are two of many issues that should be pursued by other authors.

A common thread of this monograph that highlights the challenges that lie ahead were illustrated by two of the students surveyed by Kaplan and Mable (see Chapter 2). The first student conveyed that an academic integrity code should be "communicated and celebrated," but the second professed that "I want to be the best student, no matter what it takes. Maybe it takes cheating on some occasions." The challenge for higher education is to find interventions that permit all members of the educational community to "celebrate" and value academic integrity.

CONTRIBUTORS

Dana D. Burnett, Vice President for Student Services and Dean of Students, Old Dominion University, Norfolk, Virginia

Karen O. Clifford, Assistant to the Vice President for Student Services, Old Dominion University, Norfolk, Virginia

Jon C. Dalton, Vice President for Student Affairs, Florida State University, Tallahassee, Florida

Donald D. Gehring, Director, Higher Education Program, Bowling Green University, Bowling Green, Ohio

Harold Goldsmith, Vice President for Student Affairs, Indiana University of Pennsylvania, Indiana, Pennsylvania

Wanda Kaplan, Doctoral Candidate, Old Dominion University, Norfolk, Virginia

William L. Kibler, Associate Vice President for Student Affairs, Texas A&M University, College Station, Texas

Mary E. Kite, Professor, Ball State University, Muncie, Indiana

Phyllis Mable, Vice President for Student Affairs, Longwood College, Farmville, Virginia

DONALD L. MCCABE, Associate Professor, Graduate School of Management, Rutgers University, Newark, New Jersey

GARY M. PAVELA, Director of Judicial Programs, University of Maryland, College Park, Maryland

MARY ELISABETH RANDALL, Vice President for Enrollment and Student Services, University of Maine at Augusta

LYNN RUDOLPH, Consultant, Anne Arundel Community College, Arnold, Maryland

LINDA TIMM, Vice President for Student Affairs, St. Mary's College, South Bend, Indiana

BERNARD E. WHITLEY, JR., Professor, Ball State University, Muncie, Indiana